THE
MEETING IN
THE DINER

The town of Lincoln, Ohio, was no longer the boomtown it had been in the early 1950s, back when steel was king. Peaking at 23,500 in 1954 (the year before the River Steel Corporation shut down), Lincoln's populace had fallen underneath the 18,000 imprint by the mid '70s. Nothing at any point supplanted the lucrative positions procured in the steel factory. The people who remained needed to agree to bring down paying work; you could say that they got "McDonalded."

There was additionally a period during the '50s when Lincoln High's cherished Lions were a football tradition. For evidence you can look at the glass grandstand in the corridor of the school's fundamental entry. There, gladly displayed for any kind of family down the line, are Lincoln's '50, '52, and '53 state title prizes; these cleaned bronze relics fill in as a suggestion to the local area's youngsters of its pleased legacy. Every pre-winter, old folks can be seen clustering at nearby joints and bars, thinking back with regards to bygone times—when steel was above all else and the Lions reigned supreme.

Times have since been incline in Lincoln. The factory forever shut its entryways, and the powerful Lions' thunder is nevertheless a reverberation—not one win in 24 straight excursions. Friday night's down on November 7, 1975,was probably not going to be any unique. It was the school's last round of the period, and coming to town were the Jacktown Giants, an imposing enemy intensely preferred to win their forty-second continuous game. It appeared to be inescapable that Jacktown would win another state title, making it a record four straight. Positioned the country's third best secondary school football crew by Sports Illustrated, Jacktown had outscored rivals by an edge of 37 focuses a game. Ohio sportscasters were promoting the current year's crew as the express' unequaled most prominent group. Their last customary season adversary, Lincoln, had scored just five scores during its abandoned 0–7 season.

Having been hung in likeness after the earlier week's embarrassing 28–0 misfortune to long-lasting opponent Middleburg (1–6), Coach Jack Morris completely comprehended that his training position was on the line. It made a difference minimal that in his initial training years he had twice taken the group to the state regionals. Nor, besides, did anybody care that he had been the school's double cross all-state running back in the mid 1950s. He'd had such promise then . . .

Jack Morris had been a second-group All–Big Ten halfback during his lesser year at Ohio State. As a senior, a knee injury during a scrimmage unexpectedly finished his playing profession only multi week before the beginning of the period. While Morris unemotionally acknowledged his destiny as "a component of the game," the people in Lincoln saw his sudden takeoff from the game as out and out a misfortune. All things considered, Fred Jones, the Lincoln Gazette's pro games journalist, had promoted Lincoln's beloved child for All-American distinctions and an early pick in the NFL draft.

Now in his fourteenth season as lead trainer, Jack recollected the days when he was the most well known man in Lincoln—back when he initially instructed the group was as yet perceived as a celebrated turf god. In those days, Morris might have run for city hall leader and been an obvious choice. But he had opted for a bigger job. He realized that in humble community Ohio, the townsfolk's most elevated respect went to the triumphant lead trainer. Throughout the long term, he had learned exactly how significant the triumphant piece of that title was.

It was 6:15 on Thursday morning, around 36 hours before the Lincoln-Jacktown game. Jack Morris sat alone in a stall at Abe's Lincoln Diner, perusing the Lincoln Gazette. Presently 43, Jack looked a lot of like a modest community secondary school football trainer. He wore a blue and white nylon coat that had an enormous brilliant lion decorated on the back with the words "Lincoln Lions" going through it. His matching cap displayed a similar token. On the front upper left half of his coat, little gold letters recognized him as "lead trainer," a title that should convey with it the situation with "The Man." However, on this specific morning, Coach Morris had no swagger to his walk. A 24 game losing streak doesn't by and large produce certainty, especially when you're instructing the most noticeably awful group in your school's set of experiences, and tomorrow evening you'll confront seemingly the best Ohio secondary school football crew ever assembled.

The coffee shop was a well known breakfast spot for neighborhood finance managers, regularly visited by legal counselors, bookkeepers, judges, and other Lincoln notables. At specific tables you would track down similar

inhabitants simultaneously each day of the
week's worth of work, some even on Saturdays. In spite of the fact that there
were no held tables, the standard clients realized who sat where: A gathering
of protection sales reps involved the second corner from the front entryway.
The fourth corner had a place with the investors, the fifth to the office of
business, etc. A portion of the clients had been eating at Abe's with similar
gathering of companions for a really long time, joining in the "breakfast with
the young men" custom of thousands of unassuming communities across
America. Discussions went from nearby climate conditions and legislative
issues to secondary school football. Abe Horowitz, the proprietor of the
foundation, was a self-announced games someone who is addicted, with long
stretches of sports gear decorating the cedar-framed walls.

"Up a little early earlier today, huh, Coach?" Beatrice, a ladylike server,
asked.

"Needed to beat the group," he replied. "In all honesty, with tomorrow
evening's Jacktown game, I'm not in the disposition to hear a lot of old folks
let me know how to mentor our boys."

"The manner in which those men get on your case," Beatrice said, "I'm
astounded you even come in here each morning."

"It's the espresso, Beatrice. Additionally, I for the most part don't allow
them to get to me. Be that as it may, earlier today, I figured it wouldn't
damage to arrive thirty minutes before they do."

An enthusiastic man wearing a dull suit strolled into the cafe. In his late
thirties, he was an alien to Lincoln. Scarcely any youngsters wore suits in this
present workingman's town (the more seasoned men who did obtained the
propensity during the '50s), and Jack Morris realized the individuals who did.
But it was not only the suit that tagged this man a stranger in town. He
likewise wore a late 1960s tweed snap-overflow dim and dark fedora,
complete with a red plume in the hatband. Such a cap will undoubtedly stand
out enough to be noticed. In Lincoln, baseball covers were the norm.

The man might have settled down anyplace. At the counter, a stall, or a
table. Jack Morris was the main client in the spot. But instead, the stranger
walked directly to the booth where Morris sipped on his hot coffee.

"Great morning, Coach Morris, the name is Christopher," the man
radiated, broadening his hand and finishing a good handshake. "I'm a
voyaging man going through your fine burg. I end up being a major
secondary school football fan, and I know, come Friday night, you are facing
an intense foe. I might want to help your group in the upcoming game against
Jacktown. Mind in case I go along with you for some coffee?"

"It's a free nation, and I'm not going anyplace until I finish my espresso," Morris murmured, "so grab a chair, and chill out the ground."

The more interesting plunked down. He didn't try to remove his cap. Obviously, Morris didn't see it at that point, and for what reason would it be a good idea for him to? He generally wore his cap in the diner.

After the two men traded merriments, Morris inquired, "You're not from around here, would you say you are, Mr. Christopher? If I somehow managed to figure, I'd need to say you come from the East."

"Indeed, sir," the outsider replied. "Brought up in Bethlehem, Pennsylvania. Live external Philadelphia today."

"The City of Brotherly Love," Morris said.

"Right once more, old buddy. But Bethlehem, now there's an interesting place. It's a steel town similar as Lincoln used to be. At one time Bethlehem made case to the world's biggest steel works. In any case, and significantly more fascinating in certain circles, we're better known for creating extraordinary competitors. Bethlehem is in Lehigh Valley, a genuine hotbed for reproducing big-time sports stars. Many them throughout the long term. NFL Football Hall of Fame part Chuck Bednarik is a most loved child. As are baseball's throwing legend Curt Simmons; racecar driver Mario Andretti; and heavyweight fighter Larry Holmes. All of those fine competitors hails from the Lehigh Valley."

"I know about the space's standing," Morris recognized. "I read about it sometimes in my games magazines."

"You were a significant star in your childhood," Mr. Christopher added. "I saw you play against Michigan in the Big Shoe. I wanted to cry when I previously found out with regards to your knee injury. Presently about the game tomorrow . . ."

"You said something regarding giving us help, didn't you?" Morris interfered. "You truly figure you can help us? We've been playing some really miserable football."

"You heard me right."

"What precisely would you have in care, Mr.

Christopher?" "An energy talk."

"A kick talk?"

"Truth be told. I might want to give a brief motivational speech to the group following this present evening's training," Mr. Christopher said. "I've given my

portion of motivational speeches to many secondary school and school football players, Coach. I may add that I once gave a discussion to the Philadelphia Eagles and some other chance to the Cleveland Browns. The groups I've tended to have done very well. In spite of the fact that I can't ensure a champ without fail, in any event, I can guarantee you that I'll give your young men a decent strong message that will work for them on and off the field. Indeed, sir, it will be something that will work well for them throughout the years ahead."

Trying to evaluate the more odd, Morris gazed at Mr. Christopher in wonderment. Was this individual without a doubt or some sort of a nut case?

"Don't you concur, my friend,"Mr. Christopher proceeded, "that is what instructing youngsters is genuinely about? Giving them something that will remain with them after their football days are long gone."

"You will not get a contention from me, Mr. Christopher. Nonetheless, the long haul is here and there ignored in football towns in this locale. Winning is the only thing that is important to the productive members of society of Lincoln. They treat football exceptionally in a serious way and by and by around here. It's a question of respect. As it were, it's the means by which the local area has come to characterize itself. Generally, a triumphant football crew was essential for who we were in Lincoln. The triumphant disposition worked out in a good way past the football field. It's profoundly engrained locally's way of life. Individuals around here used to trust that in case you lived in Lincoln, favorable luck came your direction since we were individuals who knew how to win. Presently, with the steel factory shut down, positions have become as scant as hen's teeth and those to be had don't pay much.

"'At least we got our incredible football custom,' individuals would say," Morris added. "But now, it's become a losing football tradition. Lincoln is at this point not tied in with winning. I'm apprehensive we view at ourselves as washouts—the blend of the helpless economy and a lackluster showing on the football field has managed this town a twofold whammy."

"Yes,my companion, I thoroughly understand Lincoln's brilliance days,"Mr. Christopher said. "Right external the valley there'd be billows of smoke in the skyline above Lincoln, and it was an indication that occasions were great. It was telling you: 'Welcome to Lincoln. Everybody is working and business is blasting.' But when the sky turned precious stone clean, maybe it were saying, 'Remain away. Business smells and everybody here is in an awful mood.'"

Glancing at his watch, Morris said, "We should return to the principle subject.

Now, you said you had a motivational speech that would assist us with whipping Jacktown?"

"Mentor, I never guarantee a success," Mr. Christopher said. "I simply don't do that. But I can promise you that I will make a positive difference in the lives of your players. I recommend we simply focus on the players, and we should not stress over the townsfolk. How about we center around how we can help those fine young men on your crew. I realize I can see them some brilliant things that will work in support of themselves. Direction that heads a long ways past the football field. Furthermore who knows, we may very well win. Didn't David kill Goliath?"

"You know, Mr. Christopher, I don't have a clue why, however something inside me lets me know you may do my young men some good."

"I guarantee you that I will, and I am a man of my statement, Coach. What time do you need me today?"

"Suppose 5:30," Morris replied, a little hesitantly. "Better believe it, be at the storage space at 5:30, Mr. Christopher."

The evening practice was routine. The players made a halfhearted effort absent a lot of energy. In spite of the fact that it stayed implicit, everybody realized that it was just a question of how much the Giants would run up the score. There was no contemplated dominating the match; all things considered, everybody was pondering how the group could "remain in the game" and hide any hint of failure. It appeared they concurred with Bill Franklin, a nearby Lincoln Gazette sportswriter who expressed, "A nearby game, say, losing by an edge of three scores or less, will be viewed as an ethical triumph for the Lions."

"My dad says that when he played for Lincoln, they generally whipped Jacktown," one player mumbled in the storage room.

"No doubt, and since the time it possesses been recompense energy for Jacktown, on the grounds that each time we're facing them they kick our butts from here to next Sunday."

A curiously large lineman raised the discussion to another level. "Who here is fearing the upcoming game however much I am?" he yelled from a standing situation on the seat, shaking his whole body to depict "the creeps" they were all feeling.

"Knock it off, you all. Here comes the coach."

Coach Morris strolled in with the outsider and remained in the storage room confronting the players. "Great practice, folks. Presently, before you head home I need you to accumulate here in light of the fact that I have an uncommon visitor today who will say a couple of words to you about the upcoming game. This is Mr. Christopher, a man who has addressed secondary school and school groups all around the Midwest. He was even acquired once to address the Cleveland Browns. Presently while he speaks, I don't need anybody opening his loud mouth." He said as he looked at the embarrassed linebacker. "I need you to show our visitor the very regard that I anticipate that you should show me."

THE PEP TALK

S till dressed in a suit,Mr. Christopher stood facing the players. He never took off his suit jacket nor did he remove his fedora. With his left hand, he held up a football in the air until there was complete silence. Then he spoke.

"There were two bison that were remaining in the open reach in Wyoming when two or three cattle rustlers riding a horse jogged by. One rancher said to the next, 'Check out those two bison. They must be the ugliest creatures on the whole range.'

"'Yeah, check out their enormous heads on their thin bodies,' the other cattle rustler said. 'What's more you know, I'm told bison are however inept as they may be ugly.'

"That is the point at which one bison said to the next bison, 'I believed that over here, home on the range,we shouldn't hear a debilitating word.'"

Several players chuckled, yet the greater part of them didn't let out a grin. The joke essentially went over their heads.

"Refined men, I caught some of you conversing with one another in the storage room,and I couldn't resist the urge to hear some of you saying some debilitating words regarding tomorrow evening's down. Of course, you are playing one staggering football crew, yet recall that they're secondary school kids—very much like you all. They're not the Ohio State Buckeyes. They're not the Cleveland Browns."

It was as though Mr. Christopher visually connected with each player in the room. Also as though as one, everyone's eyes looked down.

"The Bible tells us in Numbers part thirteen," the speaker said, "that Moses sent twelve men to the place where there is Canaan, directing them to keep an eye on the foe. 'Go up there into the slope country,' Moses taught them, 'and see what the land resembles, and regardless of whether individuals who live in it are solid or frail, whether they are not many or many.'

"Upon their return, the covert agents revealed back to Moses, 'Every one individuals we found in it are of incredible size.' They asserted that The Canaanites were enormous that in correlation they felt as little as grasshoppers. The Canaanites, in any case, were not monsters. To lead his kin into the place where there is milk and honey, Moses perceived that he should move them to see themselves deserving of having it.

"I don't see any grasshoppers in this room. In the event that you consider yourself a grasshopper, kindly lift your hand. You should, Jimmy, would you say you are a grasshopper? Or then again you over toward the back. Are you, Henry?"

"No sir," Jimmy replied, appearing to be astounded that the outsider knew his name. Henry just shook his head.

"Alright, so there are no grasshoppers in this room. I'm happy we got that out of the way.

"The Giants are not monsters. Keep in mind, men, to succeed with regards to anything, the triumphant fires up here in your mind. On the off chance that you suspect something, you rout yourself before the game beginnings. I would think you prefer not to recognize Jacktown three scores before you venture onto the field. Indeed, that is by and large what happens when you persuade yourself that you can't win.

**IN ORDER TO WIN AT ANYTHING,
THE WINNING MUST START IN YOUR HEAD.**

"In Joshua 1:9, the Bible tells us: 'Be solid and fearless; don't be scared or unnerved, for the LORD your God is with you any place you go.'"

"I rehash: Be solid. Be gutsy. Try not to be apprehensive. God is with you."

It was the second time that the outsider cited from the Bible. It appeared to stand out enough to be noticed. In any case, it was outside the current discussion. Clearly, they never heard a scriptural citation in a storage room.

"There's a tale about a Stanford math understudy who was accomplishing graduate work during the Depression," the outsider said. "His teacher declared to the class, 'Whoever scores the most elevated grade on this current

Wednesday's last assessment will be extended to the employment opportunity as my instructing assistant.'

"The understudy was monetarily tied and frantically required the task to remain in school. He concentrated so hard that he slept late upon the arrival of the test and strolled into class ten minutes late. The teacher gave him the test that comprised of eight numerical questions. Two issues were additionally handwritten

on the slate. The understudy put forth a valiant effort to finish the test, yet time expired before he found time to answer the two issues on the board.

"'I didn't have the opportunity to do those two inquiries,' he said to the teacher, highlighting the chalkboard, 'and I truly need that job.'

"'You have until Friday to turn in your responses for those two inquiries,' the educator replied, yet come Friday, that is it.'

"The grateful understudy bountifully expressed gratitude toward the educator, replicated what was composed on the slate, and headed home. He chipped away at them constantly. By Friday morning, he woke up with only two or three hours of rest, completed the test, and hurried to his educator's office with his finished assignment.

"The following morning at 7:00, the understudy heard an uproarious thump on his door.
When he went to the entryway, there stood his math professor.

"After giving him access, the teacher said, 'Congrats, you just made math history.'

"'What do you mean?'

"'Those two issues on the board,' the teacher said. 'I thought of them on the board before you showed up and let the class know that no one has at any point had the option to address them. Not even Albert Einstein. Had you been there on schedule, you would have realized they weren't essential for the test.'

"The understudy recognized that had he known reality, he couldn't ever have endeavored to answer them."

Mr. Christopher stopped for a couple of seconds to let the idea hit home. This time his crowd received the message. Heads were gesturing, and faint grins showed up on the young men's appearances. Then, at that point, he continued.

"What if you didn't know that Jacktown had a record-breaking winning streak? What if you didn't know about your team's losing streak? What if you all believed that together, there was no limit to what you can do as a team?

"No one in this room ought to ponder the past. As Carl Sandburg said, 'The past is a can of ashes.'Forget about Jacktown's series of wins. Disregard Lincoln's losing streak. Toss those contemplations crazy. Why? Since they don't make any difference. The main thing that matters when you venture onto the battleground tomorrow evening is simply the game. You got that straight, Frankie?"

Mr. Christopher tossed the football to Frank Howard,a lineman and the biggest boy on the team. He caught the ball, immediately stood to attention, and said,"Yes, sir."Mr. Christopher motioned to him to throw back the football. Howard did and sat down.

"During a new outing to Disneyland, I strolled by a play that was in progress," Mr. Christopher told the players. "The recreation area representatives asked twenty volunteers from the crowd to take an interest in the play; a mother and her five-year-old young lady were among the individuals who were raised onto the stage. The young lady didn't have a hair on her head, and she was having a great time. Her mom was having fun as much as her little girl. I discovered that they were exceptional visitors of Disney—the young lady had lost her hair since she had malignant growth and was being treated by chemotherapy. The young lady was passing on, *so for what reason would she say she were and her mom so cheerful? you might inquire*. They were so cheerful on the grounds that they were in Disneyland, that is why.

"They settled on a decision. They could feel frustrated about themselves, or they could partake in their day at Disneyland. They decided to partake in the day. They said, 'This is my day.' It was their obligation. (Incidentally, in case you separate the word liability, it signifies 'react with capacity.') Each of us needs to conclude how we will react. You can conclude how you need to react tomorrow evening. I recommend you do as that courageous young lady and her caring mother did: They concluded that they would hold onto the occasion. They decided to say, 'This is my day, and I will take advantage of it.' In the upcoming game you can decide to say, 'This is my day and I will benefit as much as possible from it.'"

THIS IS MY DAY AND I WILL MAKE THE MOST OF IT

Mr. Christopher had turned down the volume when he said, "This is my day, and I will capitalize on it," and checked out the room. He saw that a couple of the young men were heartbroken: his message was coming to them.

"Jesus showed us in John 20:29: 'Favored are the people who have not seen but then have come to believe.'

"Those were not inactive words. It's not difficult to accept that you will dominate a match when you're riding a series of wins. This evening, I am requesting that you put stock in yourselves and that you can beat Jacktown despite the fact that your previous exhibitions don't come close to theirs. This makes it harder to accept, isn't that right? I won't mess with you. It won't be simple tomorrow evening. It will be troublesome. But you can do it. Also you can begin doing it by accepting in

yourself and in your colleagues. This is the kind of thing you can begin to do at the present time. I need you all to stand up and tell the man close to you that you have confidence in him. Also I need you to explain to him why you put stock in him. Go on, do it."

Everybody stood up and turned to someone next to him and they started talking to each other. Mr. Christopher let them talk for two minutes and then he instructed them to sit back down.

"There's an anecdote around a fourteen-year-old kid who was brought into the world without a left arm. The kid let his mom know that he needed to take judo illustrations. Hesitantly she enlisted him in a course. The teacher worked with the kid, and specifically, showed him one maneuver. 'Ace this move,' the kid was told again and again.

"The kid did as he was told and before long was winning matches; he qualified to contend in the last round of a significant judo competition. His rival was a genuine animal who had predominantly crushed his adversaries. Before the match, the arbitrator pulled the educator to the side and said, 'You will get your kid killed. Regardless of whether he had two arms, he's no rivalry for this person. He's a killer.'

"'Don't stress,' the educator said. 'He'll be fine.'

"The kid even told his educator, 'I will get killed.'

"The teacher answered, 'You simply do as I showed you, and there is nothing to stress about.'

"The kid dominated the game. Returning from the competition, the kid said to his educator, 'For what reason did you release me into the ring with such a solid adversary? I don't have a left arm, and that person might have genuinely harmed me. In addition, you just trained me to dominate one action. What made you figure I could win with only one move?'

"'There is just a single guard for that move,' the teacher said, 'and that is for your adversary to snatch your left arm.'

"Do you receive the message?" Mr. Christopher asked the players. "The teacher had trained the kid to put stock all the while. Tomorrow evening, it will not be the interaction that beats you. It will be self-question. Have confidence in yourself and your partners. This is the thing that has been absent with this group. This is the thing that has caused Lincoln's current losing streak. Accept you will win. Have confidence in one another. Dispose of your doubts."

"That's right boys," Coach Morris interjected, catching on to the energy. "You can't dominate football matches on the off chance that you don't figure you can win." "Handbag Paige, the old incredible baseball player in the Negro associations, never realized how old he was," Mr. Christopher told the young men. "Everybody knew that Satchel must be older in light of the fact that he'd been pitching for such a long time. Old Satch recently continued playing and playing. At, not set in stone to know his age, a gathering of journalists encompassed him and asked, 'Satch, how old are you?'

"Handbag answered, 'In case you didn't have the foggiest idea how old you were, the means by which old would you be?'

"I offer this conversation starter to you: What sort of Lincoln group would get ready for the upcoming game assuming you had no assumptions about yourselves?"

Coach Morris filtered the eyes of his group and saw a certainty sparkling from them that he hadn't found in a long time.

"Two railroad laborers were perched on a seat," Mr. Christopher proceeded. "The leader of the organization strolled by and halted to make proper acquaintance with one of them. A while later, the other laborer said to his companion, 'I'm intrigued. How could you become such great mates with the president?'

"'He and I began for the railroad simultaneously. We worked one next to the other doing physical work,' the specialist answered.

"'But he's the president, you're as yet a laborer.'

"'Yes, I know,' he moaned. 'I came to attempt to procure $1.40 60 minutes, and he came to attempt to fabricate a railroad.'

"You see, it's everything up here in your mind," Mr. Christopher said, highlighting his temple. "Imagine yourself as a prevalent competitor playing in a great group. A triumphant group runs like an all around tuned accuracy machine with every player executing his occupation with flawlessness. Assuming you cooperate, every one of you doing precisely what you should do, you'll be a triumphant football crew. Together, this is the manner by which you can beat Jacktown."

Mr. Christopher halted to let the message hit home. There was finished quiet in the room. He walked forward and backward. Raising his voice a score, he continued.

"There was a man on a bike on a high wire above Niagara Falls. After he crossed from one side of the tumbles to the opposite side, he removed the tire and rode across on the edges as it were. The group cheered.

"'I will rehash it,' he told the crowd, 'however this time, I need a volunteer to ride on the handlebars. Who needs to volunteer?'

"No hands went up. Everybody was quiet. A young lady lifted her hand. 'I'll go with you.'

"The man put her on the handlebars and individuals began to shout, 'Don't do it. She's just a kid. How is it that you could be so remorseless? Stop.'

"The man overlooked their cries and rode across the falls, pivoted, and began to return. On his return trip, there were clearly cheers. He was a hero.

"A few columnists raced to meet the man and the little kid. One asked her, 'For what reason would you do that? You might have been killed.'

"'He's my dad,' she replied, 'and I trust him.'

"The trust of a kid. It's been said that to enter the entryways of paradise, you should accompany the trust of a child."

There was a quiet quietness in the room. No one appeared to move. It was as though time were standing still.

"Two siblings, Albrecht and Albert Dürer, lived in a little town close to Nuremberg, Germany, in the late fifteenth century," Mr. Christopher said in a voice scarcely over a whisper.

"The Dürer family was poor and had eighteen kids. The dad, a goldsmith, worked eighteen-hour days in his consistent battle to put food on the table for his enormous family. The two most established children, Albrecht and Albert, had a fantasy. The two of them needed to seek after their ability for craftsmanship. To satisfy their fantasy, they'd need to learn at the Art Academy in Nuremberg. The two young men made an agreement. They'd flip a coin, and the failure would work in the nearby coalmines, and with his income, he'd pay his sibling's method for going to the foundation. After four years, in the wake of completing his specialty studies, it would then be the victor's chance to help his sibling so he could concentrate on workmanship at the foundation. Albrecht won the throw and went to Nuremberg to turn into a craftsman. In the interim, Albert went down into the unsafe mines."

The young men inclined in, not having any desire to miss a word.

"At the workmanship institute, Albrecht was quickly perceived as a skilled craftsman. Upon his graduation, he was paid enormous expenses for his charged works. His family held a happy supper to praise his graduation on the yard of their pitiful home. Albrecht gave an impromptu speech to Albert: 'This is for you, dear sibling, since you forfeited for myself and worked in the mines. Presently it's my chance to deal with you, and you will seek after your fantasy. It is your turn to

go to the craftsmanship academy.'

"Albert stood up and with destroys streaming his cheeks, he said, 'I am so pleased and glad for you, my sibling, however I am apprehensive it is past the point of no return for me. Every one of my fingers are broken, turned, bowed, and ligament. As may be obvious, I can't return your toast since I can't get this glass, not to mention a paint brush.'

"Albrecht Dürer became one of the most popular craftsmen of his time, and today his work shows up in galleries from one side of the planet to the other. As a recognition for his sibling, he painted his sibling's busted Hands with palms together and slender fingers expanded upward. He called his drawing, *Hands*. This extraordinary magnum opus has since been renamed, *The Praying Hands*. A large number of generations have been conveyed all over the planet, and I'm certain you're comfortable with this renowned masterpiece. The following time you see a duplicate, ponder the story behind it and recall, 'No one makes it alone.'"

"We have a couple of those imploring hands on our front room divider," one of the young men spoke out."Yeah, we do as well," said another.

"We really want one another. You should go into this game and energize one another. Indeed, there will be some predicaments. This will be an extreme game. Anticipate it. They will be an extraordinary group. But you will be a great team too. You will win each play in turn. You need to anticipate that they should bring all they have. What's more in like manner, you will bring all you've got!

"You should go out there thinking, My adversary will be unbelievable *— each and every play. I will arrange Once morest him, and I will bring the best of me.* Do that, and the scoreboard and the last score will deal with itself. Rehash to yourself, *I will bring the best of me, EVERY SINGLE PLAY.* Try not to take a gander at the scoreboard. Simply center around your task, each play in turn. Again, the scoreboard and the last score will deal with itself."

"Truth be told," Coach Morris reverberated in an imposing voice. "The scoreboard and the last score will deal with itself."

"St. Peter requested a gathering from mice in paradise, 'How would you like it up here?' Mr. Christopher said.

I WILL BRING THE BEST OF ME, EVERY SINGLE PLAY.

"'We like it, yet paradise is so enormous,' one mouse answered.

"'Yeah, the spot is extremely fanned out that we truly don't get to see much of

it,' another mouse volunteered.

"'Could you give every one of us a couple of roller skates so we can get around more straightforward in paradise?' one of the mice asked.

"St. Peter said that he would, and each mouse got a couple of skates.

"A couple of days after the fact, St. Peter returned to beware of the mice, yet he was unable to track down them. He did, notwithstanding, run over an exceptionally enormous, fat, apathetic feline that had been taking a nap. St. Peter posed the feline a similar inquiry: 'How would you like it up here?'

"The feline said, 'It's awesome. The roads are fixed with gold. The sun sparkles constantly. It's lovely. Also do you know what I like the most? I love those suppers on wheels.'"

This time everyone in the room laughed. Mr. Christopher held up the football, the laughter stopped, and he continued.

"There won't be any dinners on wheels tomorrow. You can be certain that nothing will be simple. Expect the player adjusted opposite you to be the best you've at any point gone facing. Anticipate that he should be the hardest you've at any point seen. But do you know what? He's going to be up against the toughest opponent that he's ever faced. I don't need anybody to freeze. I don't need anybody to be a grasshopper. I need you to be consistent. I need you to do your best every play! Truth be told. Zero in on each play, each play in turn. What's more each time, do your best."

Mr. Christopher came to in his coat pocket. He grasped an article over his head. "Will all of you see this steel-cast reproduction of the Lincoln High School arena I'm grasping? In 1961 the River Steel Corporation made a large number of them to recognize the organization's 50th commemoration. I bet a large number of your people have one of them in plain view in your home. Lift your hand assuming your family has one."

Hands shot up in the air.

"Amazing. I'm speculating virtually every family in Lincoln should have one."

Hands were brought down and he proceeded. "All things considered, tomorrow evening, this arena will be completely filled. Every one of the 9,500 seats will be sold, and there will be much more individuals standing. As indicated by the Lincoln Gazette, a large portion of the neighborhood fans school football crew ever in the province of Ohio. Believe it or not. They're coming so they can say they saw the extraordinary Jacktown group of 1975, a group that will be discussed for a really long time to come.

"Presently there is no way around what that multitude of fans are thinking. You can't handle what's happening to them. But what you can control is what happens on a small patch of land inside this stadium. That fix of land is 100 yards in length and simply a shade in excess of 53 yards wide. I need you all to remain fixed on what you do on the battleground. This is the main thing that matters tomorrow evening. What's more course you can handle what's happening to you. To do that, you should zero in on one play at a time.

YOU CAN CONTROL WHAT'S
GOING ON IN YOUR MIND.

"To beat Jacktown, everybody should be completely centered around executing his work. Presently, you hostile linemen—every one of you has a task, and that is to dominate the container. The crate that I allude to is a three-by-three-foot region around you. That is your region when you face your adversary on the line. Your sole occupation is to hold him back from moving beyond this little space of turf. On turf, to obstruct your contradicting lineman—assuming he moves beyond you, you lose; in case he doesn't move beyond you, you win. This is your solitary obligation. Recollect now, every one of you five hostile linemen should cooperate with every one of you controlling his three-by-three-foot turf. Do this, and Lincoln will control the line. At the point when you assume responsibility for the line, you enormously improve the odds of a fruitful run, pass, or kick. In the upcoming game, your colleagues are anticipating that you should dominate your crate. They trust you will do this for them. You're not going to let them down, are you?"

This time he tossed the ball to a stocky red-headed child in the first line.

"What are you going to do, Rodney?"

Rodney Keller, a hostile watchman, stood up and yelled, "I will dominate my case, sir."Following his lead, three different linemen stood up and hollered, "I will dominate my box."

The football was gotten back to Mr. Christopher, and he proceeded. "I'm sure that everybody in this room knows about John F. Kennedy's renowned citation, 'Ask not how your nation can help you; ask how you can help your country.' I need every one of you to ask yourself, 'What would i be able to provide for the others in this room?' These are your partners. You would rather not let them down. To this end you will play your maximized operation on each down. You are doing it for them. Presently on the off chance that everybody does his best every single play, Lincoln will play its best game ever.

"In one of his most renowned talks, the Reverend Martin Luther King Jr. said to his crowd, 'In case you are a road cleaner, you should clear the roads so that the holy messengers in paradise will stop, peer down, and say, 'There goes an incredible road cleaner.'11 I need the heavenly messengers in paradise to peer down at the upcoming game and say the equivalent regarding every one of you: 'There goes an extraordinary football player.'"

Coach Morris concentrated on the appearances on his players' countenances and seen that some of them were mouthing the words, "There goes an extraordinary player." Morris had never seen such a response by a football crew. *This is stunning*, he thought to himself.

"Mohandas Gandhi cited the lessons from the exemplary Indian book Bhagavad Gita," Mr. Christopher told the group. "All through the book is the reference to the Buddhist and Hindu word dharma. It freely makes an interpretation of in English to imply that everything is the thing that it is because of nature. An illustration in the book tells about a blessed man who safeguards a suffocating scorpion in a lake. The heavenly man lifts the scorpion out of the water, and it stings him. The sting makes the man drop the scorpion, and it falls into the water. Once more, the sacred man gets it, and again he is stung, and again he drops it. This happens a few times.

"A passing rancher turns out to watch lastly asks, 'For what reason do you continue to save the scorpion when each time you do, he continues to sting you?'

"The sacred man replies, 'On the grounds that the dharma of the scorpion is to sting. It is the thing that a scorpion does.'

"'But for what reason do you continue to save it?'

"'Because it is my dharma to protect it from trouble, or for this situation, an unavoidable demise by suffocating. It is My main thing,' the heavenly man replied.

"This anecdote delineates the significance of dharma. Also tomorrow, I need every one of you to do what you're generally anticipated to do. I need you to be completely centered around each play of the game. Do that, and you'll put forth a valiant effort. You each have a task to do on each play, and

I need you to do it as well as could be expected. Why? Since THIS IS WHAT YOU DO!"

"This is My specialty," undulated unobtrusively across the storage space as a few of the players recited in scarcely discernible voices.

"some time prior, my yard was not doing so great that I called a grass care administration to treat it," Mr. Christopher said. "The following day, an organization rep went to my home, investigated my yard, and said it was past help. 'Nothing we could accomplish for it, sir,' and the man got back in his truck and drove away. Presently I've confronted dismissal before in my life, however this was whenever I first was at any point dismissed by a yard care organization. My neighbor has a pleasant yard, and I realized he experienced childhood with a ranch, so I asked him for his advice.

"'Don't stress over that person,' he said 'Simply continue to

establish grass.' "'What pretty much every one of the weeds?' I

asked.

"'Don't pull any weeds. Simply continue to establish grass. What's more be patient.'

"I did what he educated me to do. I continued to establish grass and gave no consideration to the weeds. It took some time, yet today, the grass on my yard is delightful.

"You see, it's about having a process and consistency. Mentor Morris has an interaction for you to follow. He's had one each and every season. Presently you must be steady—you need to execute it. This implies all of you. Each play in turn. Everybody plays his best. Something else: you must trust one another. This is a game with regards to trust. No one lets the group down. Everybody takes care of his business. Simply continue to establish grass. This is the means by which football match-ups are won. To beat Jacktown, it will require a whole collaboration. Is this unmistakable to everybody? Lift your hand noticeable all around assuming you get what I've quite recently told you."

Mr. Christopher brought the football up noticeable all around, and each player raised his hand.

"In case there is one thing I can guarantee you, it is that you will have affliction on the field tomorrow. Football is a game with regards to difficulty. In each play, players get wrecked, they get back up, And afterward they get thumped down once more. But you keep getting up. Having affliction is essential for the game. You acknowledge it, yet you don't permit it to overcome you. You continue to the following play. So when one of your partners faces misfortune in the game, every one of you should have one idea—you are the person who will be there for him. Realize that you will keep fixed on the interaction during the whole game, and some portion of the cycle is being there for one another. Tell all of your partners that he can trust you to go about your business. As your partner, he can trust you on each play—each play in turn. This is the way football match-ups are won. Each play in turn! Presently, I need you to all stand up again and tell one of your partners the amount you trust him and pay attention to him let you know the amount he confides in you. And

make certain to guarantee him that you won't let him down in the game tomorrow night."

The whole team stood up, and again they talked one-on-one to each other. Mr. Christopher let them talk for about two minutes. He raised the football above his head, then the talking stopped and everyone sat down.

HAVING ADVERSITY IS PART OF THE GAME. YOU ACCEPT IT, BUT YOU DON'T ALLOW IT TO DEFEAT YOU.

"During the Apollo 13 journey," Mr. Christopher said, "a blast made the van lose both fuel and oxygen on the re-visitation of Earth. Mission Captain Jim Lovell smoothly said to mission control on Earth: 'Houston, we've had an issue here.'

"There was without a doubt a difficult issue. An installed blast caused glitches that emphatically decreased the odds of the space travelers securely returning. Rather than freezing, Lovell accepted his job on the mission—ensuring he and his group returned securely. He took prompt charge of the circumstance. It didn't take a surge of adrenaline to shoot through his whole body for him to realize that the space case was in genuine peril. Lovell disregarded all interruption, and he zeroed in just on what he should do as such everybody would get by. He went right to the cycle—Lovell confided in the way that in case he remained completely centered around the interaction, they would get back securely. Tomorrow, you will zero in on each play in turn. Furthermore you will believe that this will guarantee you of a positive outcome."

Mr. Christopher stopped momentarily and strolled to the focal point of the room. "There is one more illustration to be gained from the Apollo 13 journey," he proceeded. "Furthermore that memorable is that things don't generally run as expected. There are such countless factors in an endeavor like the returning of a spaceship that you should be ready for the sudden to occur. This is valid in all undertakings, including a football match-up. In the upcoming game, you will commit errors and on occasion, your rival will dominate. Anticipate it, and when it occurs, don't be debilitate. Disregard the keep going play, and spotlight on the current play. Furthermore when things aren't turning out well for you, don't permit yourself to become discouraged."

Mr. Christopher tossed the ball to Johnny Corleone.

"You're the quarterback, Johnny. I need you to tell your partners what

you will do assuming that you get sacked or toss an
interception."

Corleone, an alluring, slender kid, stood up. Despite the fact that he looked athletic, his slight form appeared to be more appropriate for a ball court than the football field. All things considered, he talked with a peaceful certainty, and from the response of different players, he was obviously a group chief. "It's just one play," he said, cautiously picking his words, "and I'm not going to allow it to get to me. I'll let myself know that I will improve next time."

"Generally excellent, Johnny,"Mr. Christopher gestured approvingly.

"Winston Churchill was once approached to convey a beginning discourse to the young men of an old tuition based school," he proceeded, "and his message was important for the two its reality and its curtness. The incomparable British top state leader moved toward the platform, confronted his crowd and said: 'This is the illustration: never yield, never surrender—never, never, never, never, in nothing incredible or little, huge or unimportant, never give in but to feelings of honor and capable. Never respect power; never respect the obviously overpowering may of the enemy.'

NEVER GIVE IN, NEVER GIVE IN, NEVER, NEVER, NEVER . . .

"Having said these couple of words, Churchill left the platform. It's plausible that no one in the crowd at any point failed to remember his message. He might have represented an hour and not have had such an impact.

"This evening I rehash, 'Never, never, never yield.' There will be times when you are down in the upcoming game, yet you should never capitulate to overcome. Recollect that no one—not one man in this room—gives in tomorrow evening. You play collectively, and you win as a team.

"Never, never yield," Corleone rehashed for all to hear.

"A mother was stressed over her little child who was late returning home from school,"Mr. Christopher said. "When the young man at long last strolled in the entryway, she tensely said to him, 'Where have you been? I was really anxious about you.'

"'There was another young man and his bike was bankrupt,' he told her, 'so I needed to help him.'

"'Hey,wait a moment, young fellow,' she said. 'You know nothing about fixing bicycles.'

"'I know,' the young man replied. 'I needed to plunk down and help him cry.' "Tomorrow, you're all going to be there for one another. You are going to help one another. You will be centered all together."

Mr. Christopher stopped. There was a quiet in the room as everybody stood by to hear what the outsider would say next.

"A companion of mine once informed me regarding his childhood, pondering how he recalled his dad. As a young man, subsequent to getting back from the supermarket with his dad, he had a comic book in his pocket.

"'Where did you get that?' the dad inquired. "'I took it from the basic food item store.'

"The dad communicated his failure and returned to the store to pay for it. After seven days, the kid got back home with one more comic book from the supermarket. At the point when the dad saw it, he inquired, "Where did you get that?" The kid told him, and once more, the dad said that isn't right to take, and he returned to the store and paid for it.

"A third time, the kid took another comic book, and this time the dad put the kid over his knee and hit him. It was the solitary time he had at any point struck his child, my companion told me.

"'That was the last time I at any point took anything,' my companion explained.

"'So by getting punished you taken in a decent illustration and that is the thing that prevented you from taking?' I asked.

"'No. What halted me was a short time later,' my companion said. 'Hearing my dad cry outside my room in the passage—that is the thing that halted me.'

"I believe there's a decent upright here with regards to mindful and trusting. Realizing that your colleagues care about you and trust you is the thing that is important in the upcoming game. It's additionally concerning how you care about them and how you trust them. You should trust your partners as a whole. Everybody here adds to the outcome. On the off chance that you don't confide in one another, you don't confide in anyone."

Mr. Christopher threw the ball to Mark Mitchell, who was sitting in the focal point of the room. While not especially enormous, Mitchell was strong.

"Great catch, Mitch," the speaker said. "Obviously, you're a linebacker so you're relied upon to remain fixed ready—and incidentally, it's alright assuming that you get a couple of tomorrow evening. Presently what's the significance here to you?"

I WILL DO MY BEST TO LIVE UP
TO THEIR EXPECTATIONS.

Mitchell stood up and said, "Sir, I realize my colleagues trust me to play my most impressive showing of all time. Also that is actually the thing I will do. Realizing that they trust me implies that I can't let them down—I will give a valiant effort to satisfy their hopes. That is a guarantee, sir."

Mitchell passed the football back. Mr. Christopher looked Mitchell in the eye and nodded his head in approval. "I have full confidence in you, son." He then continued. "I'm reminded about another little boy who was upset with his parents and ran away from home. He packed two cans of root beer, two Twinkies, and went to the park. He sat down on a park bench next to an old woman to have one of his Twinkies and a root beer. He offered her a Twinkie, and she accepted it. Then he gave his other root beer to her, and she took it too. After he finished, he decided to go home and walked away. He took a few steps, turned around, walked back to the old woman and gave her a hug. She gave him a warm smile.

"When the young man got back, his mom asked him about his day and for what valid reason he was so cheerful. 'I just met God in the recreation area,' he replied, 'and she had the most wonderful smile.'

"The older lady returned home and her child asked her with regards to her day and for what good reason she was so glad. 'I just met God in the recreation area,' she replied, 'and He's much more youthful than I suspected He would be.'"

Coach Morris concentrated on the players' countenances and was astonished to see a couple of tears. He saw a lineman put his arms noticeable all around as though to yawn, and as he brought down his right arm, he cleaned his eyes. *This Mr. Christopher is great*, the mentor thought to himself.

"The anecdote about the little child and old lady is about affection. In John

15:12, Jesus said, 'This is my edict, that you love each other as I have cherished you.' Note that Jesus didn't propose or request that we love one another. He told it. I need every one of you to cherish one another. Since when you love someone else, you need to put forth a valiant effort for him. You additionally believe that individual. Trust each man in this group and accept that he will go about his business on Friday night."

"Trust," Morris said in an uproarious voice for accentuation. A significant number of the players reacted by rehashing, "Trust."

"Winning in life is tied in with really focusing on others and accepting in them,"Mr. Christopher continued. "You need to have faith in the process in the upcoming game. You should have trust. You need to believe that Coach Morris will settle on the ideal choices on which players are placed into the game and what plays are called. You need to trust one another. You should believe that every one of your partners will take care of his task on each play—very much like you will do yours for them. Believe that no one will let you or the group down. Have faith in one another. You trust since you care about one another. Recollect that. Presently for what reason do you trust each other?"

"In light of the fact that we care about one another," the group shouted.

"Indeed, you care for one another, and on the grounds that you

love one another." "Indeed, in light of the fact that we love one

another," Corleone shouted.

Mr. Christopher continued. "In Mark 11:24, we are told:

'Whatever you request in petition, accept that you have gotten it, and it will be yours.'

"I need you to accept that Lincoln will beat Jacktown tomorrow evening. I need you to paint a clear picture to you that Lincoln has dominated the match. Envision what you should do in each play to get it going. Request it, have confidence in it, and it will happen."

Mr. Christopher halted to allow the players to process what he said. Pacing back and forth, he then said, "There is a story about the late Martin Luther King Jr., who was sitting toward the rear of the transport and saying to himself: 'I might stroll to the rear of the transport, however I left my psyche toward the front of the transport. One day I will put my body up there where my brain is.'

"Do you see what conviction and petition can achieve? Instead of feeling bittering and angry, Dr. Lord envisioned a positive idea. It was a picture of what he imagined would be later on and a dream that he requested in supplication. Then he worked to make his prayer come true.”

Mr. Christopher held the football high over his head and stood by again for complete quiet. He then said, “I’ll wrap this up now by asking each of you to say a prayer tonight before you go to sleep. In your supplication, request God that you and all from your partners play as well as could be expected. Let God know the amount you trust all of them, and request that he assist you with being centered around each play. Likewise supplicate that no one, including your rivals, is harmed in the game. Do this, and put stock in your supplication. What you request will be yours.

“God favor you.”

A grave calm occupied the room. Not at all like past motivational speeches, no one commended. Nor were there any high fives. Truth be told, no one said a word for a few long minutes. At long last Coach Morris ended the quiet. “Alright, folks, that is it for this evening. Recollect now, lights off by 9:30; I need you all to get a decent night’s rest so you’ll be all around rested for tomorrow’s game.”

After the last player had left, Coach Morris asked an associate, “I’m searching for Mr. Christopher. Have you seen him anywhere?”

“Say, who right? Also how could he realize every one of the players’ names?” the associate mentor asked.

“I’ll make certain to ask him that when I converse with him,” Morris replied. “Where is he?”

“He took off following he wrapped up talking,” the associate mentor replied. “Sure appeared to be in a hurry.”

THE LINCOLN-
JACKTOWN GAME

Driving on the interstate, Mr. Christopher turned the dial on his radio and tuned into the game. He glanced skyward and said, “It’s showtime.”

“It’s standing room only here in Lincoln, Ohio,” the voice on the radio said. “This is a 9,500-seat stadium, but there must be 12,000 fans here tonight. This crowd brings back memories from the ’50s, when the Lions were a real powerhouse. That’s when Jack Morris was Lincoln’s great running back. Mr. Reliable, Number 13. Here's a bit of trivia, sports fans: Guess whose number is the only one ever retired by Lincoln High School? Yes, that's right, folks, Jack Morris's number, the same Jack Morris who is Lincoln's present head coach. The way the team has been losing games, though, this could very well be his last season. I understand he sells real estate in the off-season. Don't give up your part-time sales job, Jack.

"The opposing group has swaggered onto the field. Kid, they look huge. The group is giving them an overwhelming applause. It's been this way every season. The Giants are getting the regard that is expected them. They are without a doubt one of the best secondary school groups in Ohio history. Positively the best this commentator has ever seen.

"Presently here comes the Lincoln Lions . . . I don't trust it; the group scarcely mixed. Some fans are cheering them on, but nothing like what we just heard when the Giants came out—I'm even hearing some booing. Presently, that is definitely wrong. It doesn't matter to me the number of games the Lions have lost. They are the old neighborhood group, and we should not neglect, they're secondary school kids. I'm truly baffled in the helpless sportsmanship just showed by these fans. It's simply not called for. After this declaration, I'll be back with the kickoff."

The band played "The Star-Spangled Banner," and after the coin throw the host said, "Lincoln won the throw and has chosen for kick. I don't get it. Assuming I were Coach Morris, I'd need to keep the ball out of the Giants' hands.

Especially their extraordinary running back, Billy Thomas—he certainly gets my decision in favor of the current year's Mr. Football in Ohio. He has 21 scores and 1,865 hurrying yards. Well that is the thing that I call a great deal of land, sports fans.

"Number 1, Josh GoldMan, is the Lions' place kicker. He kicks the ball and it's gotten by Billy Thomas on the 20. There is a multitude of blue outfits around the speedster at the 30. I see one missed tackle, two, no make that three missed handles. Thomas gets through, and he's in the open. Also no one will get him. Man, that kid can fly. He's at the 30, the 20, the 10—score. We're ten seconds into this game and it's Jacktown, 6; Lincoln, zip. This group is awestruck. They came to see the best group in the land, and they won't be denied. For sure. Billy Thomas must be the best running back in secondary school football. I'll set him facing anybody. Indeed sir, anybody. You can make certain there are school scouts in the stands each time Jacktown takes the field—stand by one second, people. A banner is on the field. The ref is showing that the Giants were offside on the opening shot.

They're getting back to the score back. Lincoln will kick again from their 45-yard line. We'll stop for a commercial."

"Yes," said Mr. Christopher, shutting out a business. "Go Lions." "Josh

Goldman kicks The ball, however it's off the side of his foot. The ball takes a bob on the Jacktown 40-yard line," the host says. "A terrible

kick. The ball is free. There is a multitude of players with both red and blue pullovers around the ball. Also pause . . . the blue group has concocted the ball! What about this one, avid supporters? Josh Goldman has recuperated his own kick! The Lions have the ball on the Jacktown 38-yard line. Someone up there should like the Lions. You don't regularly see the spot kicker muff the ball and afterward recuperate it. But as the saying goes, folks, that's the way the ball bounces.

"Johnny Corleone takes the snap and tosses a shot pass to his tight end. It's gotten and the Lions have the ball on the 26-yard line. First down for Lincoln."

Three running plays moved the ball to the 18-yard line. "It's fourth and 2 yards for the Lions, and Josh Goldman is in to endeavor the field objective. He has made four of every eighteen endeavors this season, his longest just 21 yards. This will be a 34-yard kick. The ball is snapped, it's noticeable all around . . . it's benefit! Lincoln gets on the board first. What about that! We're three minutes into this game and Lincoln is beating Jacktown, 3–0. The Giants don't appear to be

even the slightest bit stressed, people. Truth be told, I figure the Lions may have quite recently made them frantic. Trust me on this one—the last thing you need to do is fire up a group any semblance of Jacktown."

On the opening shot, the ball was gotten on the 20-yard line by Jimmy Sims and was gotten back to the 40-yard line. "The Giants will begin their own 40 with great field position," said the host. "In the event that you just tuned in, we're just minutes into this game, and it's 3 to flash for the Lions. Truth be told, people, you heard it right. It's Lincoln, 3; Jacktown, 0.

"First and 10, and the ball is given to Billy Thomas. He takes the ball off right tackle and is down in Lions' domain on the 46-yard line. A simple initially down for the Giants.

"Alright, it's First and 10 on the 46. Tony Scala takes the snap and tosses a speedy ignore only the focal point of the line, and it is wrecked by Mark Mitchell. Great protective play for the Lions' linebacker. The Giants break the cluster, line up, and Scala tosses a pass to his tight end. It's a finish, and Jacktown has the ball at the 33-yard line. First and 10.

"The Giants attempt an opposite with Scala giving the ball off to Sammy

Pittman. He's hit by linebacker Mark Mitchell for a 6-yard misfortune. That is two phenomenal guarded plays for Mitchell in this drive.

"The Giants start on the 39-yard line. The ball is given to Billy Thomas who conveys it to the 29-yard line, a get of ten for the exciting halfback. It's third and 6, and Thomas again gets the ball; he cuts wide around the left half of the line, and he gets five additional yards.

"It's fourth and 1 on the 24-yard line, and doubtlessly the Giants will put it all on the line. The ball is snapped, and Scala runs into a mass of blue. He goes no place. The Lions halted him cold, and they take over on their own 24-yard line. Would you be able to trust it? This host group swarm likes what they see. The fans give a major acclaim for the guarded unit as they stroll off the field. I can see Coach Morris down there, high-fiving his protective players on the sidelines."

On the following series, the Lions ran a blend of passing and running plays. Quarterback Johnny Corleone finished four out of seven passes, and Lincoln moved the ball to Jacktown's 38-yard line. It's fourth down, 2 yards.

"They're acquiring Josh Goldman to dropkick," the commentator says. "The ball is snapped, and Goldman dropkicks a high kick that ricochets on the 11-yard line. Blue outfits swarm around the ball; it's rolling, rolling, and it stops on the

one-yard line where Lincoln downs it. It's first and 10 on the 1-yard line for the Giants. Who might have at any point envisioned? We'll be back after a message from our sponsors."

Mr. Christopher laughed as he passed during that time with the radio on maxing out. "Remain on track, Lions. Trust in yourselves. Trust each other."

STAY FOCUSED.

On the principal play, Pittman conveyed the ball up community for a 1-yard gain. The following play, Thomas was halted on the 4-yard line by Mark Mitchell. On third down, Giants quarterback, Tony Scala, tossed a pass that was gotten and dropped because of a hard hit by Mitchell. The Giants had to kick from their end zone on fourth down. Lincoln took over on the 44-yard line. "Lincoln has extraordinary field position, and there's not even a shadow of a doubt, people, the Lions are in this ball game, late in the main quarter. By George, they're even ahead."

On the following series, Johnny Corleone finished five passes, getting three first downs, with the ball winding up on the Jacktown 4-yard line. The following three plays were two runs that neglected to create any yardage and a missed pass in the end zone. "That one was almost taken out by the Giants," the host said, "and had he made the catch, he would have gone above and beyond. It's presently fourth down, four seconds on the clock in the main quarter, and Josh Goldman is coming in to endeavor the field objective. I remind you, parents, that the Giants have obstructed nine this season, a state record. Here is the snap, the Giants are charging. Goldman gets the kick not yet decided, and . . . it's benefit! The Lions lead 6 to 0! Pay attention to that group! They're truly into this game at this point. The primary quarter has finished, and the Lions are on top. Six to zip. We'll be correct back."

Both groups moved the ball all over the field in the subsequent quarter, however there were no focuses put on the board. With 26 seconds left at work before the half, Scala finished a 50-yard pass to Sammy Pittman who was constrained outside the alloted boundaries on the 9-yard line. Billy Thomas ran up the center for 2 yards, and the Giants called a break with fifteen seconds staying on the clock. The Giants arranged rapidly and tossed a pass, yet it was wrecked by Mark Mitchell in the end zone. On third down, Scala attempted a quarterback sneak and was halted on the 1-yard line. The Giants called an opportunity to stop the clock.

"It's fourth down, and Jacktown is behind 6–0," the host said. "With three seconds left in the principal a large portion of, the Giants have the ball on the 1-yard line. *Remember they haven't been closed out for a whole a large portion of every season.* Scala gets the ball, he hands off to Thomas. A major opening in the line opens on the right side, and he scores. The score is tied 6–6." The Giants made the additional point and they were ahead 7–6 at the half.

"Lincoln has figured out how to remain in this ballgame," the host said. "The Giants lead by one. It's been quite a while since any group has tested them like this. The inquiry is, would lincoln be able to keep it up? The Giants have outscored their rivals by 26 in the subsequent half. They are enormous, and they are solid. They are an all around focused group and in phenomenal state of being. Will they wear out the more modest Lincoln Lions during the subsequent half ? It's profoundly plausible. But you've got to give credit to the Lions and their head coach, Jack Morris, for putting up a terrific first half. Also what about their quarterback, Johnny Corleone, with eleven consummations in seventeen endeavors? All through the whole 1975 season, no quarterback has had ten culminations against Jacktown. Also what's more great is that Corleone has just been sacked once. Taking into account the amount they are outsized by the Giants, Lincoln's hostile line is holding up very well.

"And on the opposite side of the ball (is the way that) linebacker Mark Mitchell has twelve handles, two sacks, and he's split up five passes. What a first half for Mitchell! The person midpoints four handles a game! Also what might be said about that Number 1, Josh Goldman? In addition to the fact that he has two field objectives, he recuperated his own opening shot that set up the Lions' first score.

"The central issue is, can the Lions keep up this exhibition in the second half against the Jacktown Giants, a group that is undefeated in their last 41 games, and a three-time state champion? Can the winless Lincoln Lions keep on playing with a similar degree of power for the whole game? Recall now, it was simply last Friday night when a powerless Middleburg shut out the Lions 28–0. I promise a certain something—the whole arena here in Lincoln is thinking about what in the world Coach Jack Morris did to get his group so started up ...Well, don't disappear, people. Maybe we may very well have ourselves a typical barnburner here this evening in Lincoln, Ohio."

Driving down the highway, a fired up Mr. Christopher said, "Alright, Coach, there are as yet two quarters left in this game," similarly as though he were in the storage space conversing with Jack Morris. "Tell your young men that the Jacktown Giants

are not goliaths all things considered. You're directly in this game. Tell them how well they're doing and since they remained with Jacktown for the principal half, they can rehash it for the following half. Tell your group that they can win it. Remind them to keep on track. Disregard the scoreboard. Each man executes his task, and everybody believes that every one of his partners will go about his business. Trust. Trust in one another. Advise your hostile linemen to dominate their container. Simply continue to establish grass. Everybody plays his best game. You win each play in turn. Let them know what we are told in Mark 11:24, 'Whatever you request in petition, accept that you have gotten it, and it will be yours.' And another thing, Coach, have them say a supplication before the beginning of the second half."

Meanwhile, in the storage space, the players' heads were down while every kid said a quiet prayer.

"Alright, folks," Coach Morris said, "we should go out and improve for the following portion of the game. We've demonstrated that we are a commendable adversary, and the Jacktown group knows they're facing an impressive enemy. Keep in mind: remain on track and disregard the scoreboard. It's each play in turn. I need every one of you to go about his business. What's more trust that your colleagues will do theirs. We should do it!"

The started up Lions ran onto the field to an overwhelming applause, a tough invite that a Lincoln group had not gotten for some years.

"The two groups are back on the field for the second 50% of this astonishing game," the commentator said. "The score is 7–6. The amazing Jacktown Giants are up by a solitary point. The persistent Lions are setting up a fierce battle. No one in this state anticipated such a nearby game. But we still have two more quarters of football to play, and as we know, the Jacktown Giants know how to put points on the scoreboard in the second half. The subsequent half is going to begin. We'll find out."

Mr. Christopher listened eagerly to the whistle flagging the second 50% of play, however at that point his radio started to get a ton of static. He tracked down another station with perfect timing to get the start of the half.

"There's the opening shot, and Vinny Tarantino takes it on the 15-yard line. He runs up the middle, he breaks one tackle, and he's hit on the 30-yard line. The Lions are looking great so far in this subsequent half, folks."

The Lincoln group made two first downs, yet in the wake of moving into Jacktown domain had to dropkick from the 42-yard line. Josh Goldman drop-kicked a high spiraling kick, and Billy Thomas motioned for a reasonable catch on the 10-yard line.

"The Jacktown offense takes the field without precedent for this subsequent a large portion of," the host said. "Keep in mind, this is a focused, very much molded football crew. To be perfectly honest, I'm not sure how Lincoln can hold them under control. These Giants are just too great a ball team."

Static on Mr. Christopher's radio indeed overwhelmed the commentator. He turned the dial, changing from one station to another, however could presently don't get the game. "Recollect young men," he mumbled to himself. "Trust. Each play in turn. Ace the case. Have confidence in yourselves. You are not grasshoppers. You can do it."

Some time later,Mr. Christopher had headed to the edges of Cleveland, where he attempted once more—this time effectively—to get the game on his radio. "This is WHHO-AM communicating what will be forevermore referred to here in Lincoln as 'The Game.'Folks, this is Ohio secondary school football in its best hour. There are 42 seconds staying on the clock and Lincoln is upheld somewhere down in its own region. The ball is on the 12-yard line. The clock is halted with an incompleted pass. The score stays 7–6, and the Lions have one break remaining. It's fourth down and the Lions are making it work. Jack Morris sends the play. Corleone returns into the pocket close to his end zone. He's being blitzed and he tosses a speedy pass to the sidelines that's

. . . gotten by Vinny Tarantino! Tarantino races down the sidelines. There's no one close to him! He's actually going, going, and he crosses into Jacktown domain. Here comes one player, Ricky Jones, to stop him. Jones powers Tarantino too far out at the 40-yard line. Thirty seconds stay on the clock! What a mind boggling hostile play under huge strain! That is number twenty for Johnny Corleone. What a record night he's having! He's twenty for 28. The group is on its feet going wild! Nobody has left this arena this evening; indeed, it seems like more have come as the expression of this conceivable surprise spread!

"OK, the Lions line up with Corleone in the shotgun. He gets the snap. He's under a ton of strain. He tosses the ball, and the pass is separated on the 25-yard line. The clock shows 21 seconds remaining."

"Come on, Johnny," Mr. Christopher yelled. "You can do it."

"There's most likely enough an ideal opportunity for one, perhaps two passes. A field objective will dominate this match, however they're not in field-an objective area. The ball is snapped and the barrage is on. Corleone can't track down a collector. He gets out of the pocket; no one is open. He tracks down an opening in the focal point of the field. He keeps the ball. He loosens up and is hit hard at the 30-yard line. The clock is down to three seconds as Lincoln calls its last time-out.

"Mentor Morris is conversing with his players. They're back on the field and Morris has sent in Josh Goldman to endeavor the field objective. Goldman has two for the evening, and this one will be from the 35-yard line, a 45-yard field-objective endeavor. I'm informed that Goldman has never kicked one from this distance in a game, not even in a training. This one would come down on even Lou 'the Toe' Groza, the Browns' incredible kicker, maybe everything the game has ever seen."

"You can do it, Josh,"Mr. Christopher hollered out the window. "Come on, line. Try not to allow this one to get blocked."

"What a game! Indeed sir,we have a genuine barnburner this evening," the host proceeded. "The ball is at the 30-yard line, What's more Goldman will endeavor to kick it from the 35. There's a break on the field. Jacktown's last break. They need to ice Goldman. Presently here's a come child into this evening's down with precisely what you'd call an amazing field-objective list of qualifications. He's never made two field objectives in a solitary game. Presently he's going for his third field objective in this game and endeavoring the longest field objective of his life in the greatest round of his life. Talk about pressure. And Goldman, a senior, is scarcely seventeen years of age. Alright, they're back on the field. The two groups line up and face each other on the 30. Here comes the snap. The ball is down, Goldman kicks it, and the ball is noticeable all around. It's anything but a high kick, and it's going toward the right half of the goal line. I couldn't say whether it has sufficient power behind it . . . The ball hits the right half of the goal line. It bounce back vertical toward the left. It's benefit! It's benefit! Lincoln overcomes the undefeated Giants, 9–7! What a game! What a win!

"Would you be able to accept that Goldman did it? However, let me let you know people, Goldman endured a hard shot after the ball was noticeable all around by Number 63, all-state 260-pound tackle Henry Greene. Greene just evened out him. There's a banner on the field for roughing the kicker, however Lincoln isn't going to take the punishment. This game is finished. It's in the set of experiences books. We've recently seen the greatest bombshell in Ohio secondary school football. You heard it right, people. It's Lincoln, 9; Jacktown, 7.

Jacktown's 41 game series of wins has finished. Furthermore goodness indeed, people, so has Lincoln's 24 game losing streak.

"This group is happy. What a ballgame. I've seen nothing like it. The Lincoln Lions have quite recently crushed the beforehand unbeaten Jacktown Giants. Indeed, you heard that right people. Lincoln, 9; Jacktown, 7.

"The fans have raged the field. There will be a major festival in Lincoln, Ohio, this evening. It will be quite a while before they disregard this one."

AFTER THE BIG GAME AND WHATEVER HAPPENED TO . . . ?

There was much joy in Lincoln, Ohio, after the Lions' big victory over the Jacktown Giants. A late-afternoon Saturday special edition of the *Lincoln Gazette* was dedicated to The Game. The headlines boldly stated: "LINCOLN WINS GREATEST FOOTBALL GAME EVER PLAYED." The caption was less exaggerated, asserting: "Lions Whip Giants in Colossal Upset."

Main articles adorned the individual Herculean physicality, including

Lincoln's three star entertainers. One article was named: "Kicker Josh Goldman, Number 1, Outscores Jacktown with 9." Only a solitary sentence in the extended article referenced that a late hit had made Josh Goldman experience a messed up femur in the last play of the game. A subsequent article read in striking print: "Imprint Mitchell: Breaks up 11 Passes, Has 24 Tackles." A third article proclaimed the quarterback; its title read: "Johnny Corleone Completes 20 out of 29." There was likewise an anecdote concerning how three of the group's seniors had the round of their lives. The story's title read: "Lincoln Says Farewell to Three Courageous Lions: Corleone, Mitchell, and Goldman."

The Lincoln Gazette additionally adulated Coach Jack Morris, old Mr. Reliable, who came through in the greatest round of his whole vocation—remembering his playing days for the '50s when he featured at Lincoln High School and later at Ohio State.

There had been gossip that Coach Morris would be terminated toward the year's end. After the Jacktown triumph, no one at any point set out to raise the subject of terminating Jack Morris. His saint status had returned, and by and by, he was the most well known man in Lincoln, Ohio. He kept on selling land throughout the mid year months, and despite the fact that he just worked at it low maintenance, he sold more land than some other specialist in the whole county.

In February, Johnny Corleone broke his collarbone and right arm in a cruiser mishap and never played football again. Josh Goldman's leg recuperated, however he never again kicked another football. Mark Mitchell graduated and went to Ohio State where he studied money. He played intramural football for his fraternity.

In July 1976, after Johnny Corleone's graduation, the Corleone family moved to Toledo, where his dad Tony Corleone found a new line of work as an assembly line laborer at the Jeep factory.

Josh's dad, Harry Goldman, proprietor of Goldman's Clothiers, a men's store on Main Street in midtown Lincoln, had turned into a survivor of the local area's difficult situations. Following 35 years in business, Harry Goldman unexpectedly maintained a leaving business deal in August 1977 and shut down his store until the end of time. The GOB deal concurred with the termination of his rent. That very year, the family moved to Cleveland Heights where Harry Goldman went to work for his brother by marriage who claimed a discount food company.

After moving on from Ohio State as a money major, Mark Mitchell accepted a position with State National Bank in Columbus, Ohio. After a progression of acquisitions, State National became one of the biggest territorial banks in the United States. Having been on the bank's most optimized plan of attack and following a progression of advancements, Mark Mitchell was named CEO in 2001. His dad, Bill Mitchell, a single man, stayed in Lincoln where he filled in as an independently employed house painter. In 1992, Bill Mitchell experienced a lethal heart attack.

Johnny Corleone went to Bowling Green State University in Bowling Green, Ohio, only forty miles south of Toledo, where he studied designing. After school he moved to Boston to work for a little innovation organization. In a little while, alongside two colleagues, he helped to establish Alpha Technology. The organization turned out to be immensely fruitful and was recorded on the New York Stock Exchange. Johnny was subsequently named executive of the board and CEO.

Josh Goldman moved on from Wittenberg University in Springfield, Ohio, hitched his school darling, and turned into a secondary school history instructor in Dayton, Ohio, his significant other's old neighborhood. He likewise instructed the kid's soccer team.

During their childhood in Lincoln, the three young men had just been easygoing companions and didn't keep in contact after high school.

PRE-REUNION

On the afternoon of Tuesday, September 28, 2003, John Corleone paced his plush office talking on his headset. "That's right, Bill, I'll be serving as the board chairman of the hospital concurrently with my remaining term as chair of the United Way board," the physically fit forty-four-year old chief said.

"You're really amazing," reacted the voice on the opposite finish of the telephone. "With regards to rewarding this local area, I don't think I've at any point heard you say no."

"All things considered, it resembles we're told in Luke 12:48, Mayor," Corleone proceeded. "To whom much has been given, a lot will be required."

"And as I like to say, my old buddy, assuming that you need something done, you give it to a bustling man. Have an incredible day, John."

"You as well, Your Honor."

Upon hanging up, the voice on the intercom said, "Mr. Corleone, I have a woman holding on line three. She wants to talk to Johnny Corleone. I've told her several times that you're tied up, but she said it's urgent and she'd wait. It's Margaret Morris."

"I don't perceive the name. Who's she with?"

"Said it was close to home. Said to let you know she's Jack Morris' wife."

"I ought to have known," Corleone replied. "No one's called me Johnny since I left Lincoln. Talk about a name from an earlier time. Indeed, by all means put her through."

"Hi, Mrs. M," Corleone said. "I am sorry for keeping you on hold." "I was apprehensive you wouldn't recall who I was."

"It's been quite a while, ma'am. Haven't seen you and Coach since my mother's memorial service back in '89, a year after we lost my dad. However, certain I recall you. How are you and Coach Morris doing these days?"

"He's actual debilitated, Johnny. Has a mind growth, and the specialist says it's inevitable. Could be any day."

"Gracious, I'm so grieved," Corleone answered. "You know it's been a long time since I've seen Coach. I actually picture him unshakable."

"Well Johnny, he's beyond seventy now and had been looking extraordinary. As of not long ago, that is. Then he started getting these awful headaches about two years ago," Margaret Morris said in a soft voice. "He's been in and out of the Cleveland Clinic, and presently they say there is nothing they can do. We can just ask. Specialists say it's just an issue of half a month. Jack has mentioned that I call three of his previous players. You, Josh Goldman, and Mark Mitchell. He would like you all to come here. Jack said he needs to converse with you young men. I realize it sounds emotional, similar to one of those deathbed scenes you find in the motion pictures. His definite words were, 'Tell the young men that it's urgent.'"

Margaret Morris' voice tore up; she battled to proceed. "We've been following your vocation, Johnny, and we're both so glad for you. For your work, however your municipal and beneficent exercises. What's more normally we know about how bustling you are."

"Is Coach lucid?"

"Not generally. I'd need to say in and out. I can't guarantee you that he'll have the option to converse with you. However, he's clear now, and he demanded me calling you."

"When mentors need every one of us to be there?" Corleone interjected.

"I realize this is without prior warning, yet would you be able to be here this Friday?" Margaret Morris murmured in a delicate hush.

"Hang on a sec, and I'll check," Johnny said, and confronting his radio he stood up: "Katie, I want you to get my schedule so I can see what's on my plan for Friday."

Katie Wilson, a chunky moderately aged chief partner, gone into the room. She gave a piece of paper to her chief. "You have three committee meetings in the morning, you know, the usual ones, then lunch with Fred Benson, and at 2:00, the company helicopter is scheduled to take you to the Cape. You have a blended pairs tennis match-up with Liz and the Meyers at 4:30. On Saturday, you have your customary golf match-up at the club at the Cape."

After looking at his timetable, Corleone said, "Mrs. M, are you still there?"

"I'm here, Johnny, and I couldn't resist the urge to hear what your secretary was saying. Seems like Friday will not work."

"What time would you like me to be there, Mrs. M?"

Margaret Morris said with a shocked ring in her voice, "Assuming that you could be here before early afternoon on Friday."

"Will do, Mrs. M."

"Katie, help Me out and drop everything for this Friday," Corleone told his associate. "I'll actually call Liz. Gosh, I would rather not baffle her. Oh yes, please tell Ted I'll need the company jet on Friday morning. Mrs. M, you still there? Great. Katie is getting on the line. Katie, please get the address, phone number, and directions to their house from Mrs. M."

A similar evening, Mark Mitchell looked immediately at the name and telephone number that his secretary left around his work area. Meanwhile, he meditatively concentrated on the horizon of downtown Columbus from his extensive office on the highest level of the State National Bank building. The message had evoked recollections from his childhood. It was an excellent pre-winter day. *My cherished season and an ideal day for football*, he verbally processed as he dialed the number.

"Morris home," addressed a delicate lady's voice.

"Mrs. M, This is Mitch—Mark Mitchell—returning your call. How are you?"

"Hello, there, Mitch, it's great to hear your voice." "How's Coach Morris?"

"That is the reason I called. Bad. Mentor has a broken cerebrum growth. Been in and out the most recent few weeks," Margaret Morris said, her voice breaking. "The specialist says that Coach will not associate with much longer."

"Please accept my apologies," Mitchell reacted. "I'm so sorry."

"I know, Mitch. We as a whole are. Everyone loves Jack. Presently the explanation I called you, Jack requested that I call three individuals whom he demands conversing with before he passes. You're one of them. He'd mentioned that you come here this Friday. He says it's very important."

"I haven't conversed with Coach in such countless years, Mrs. Morris. To tell you the

truth, it's been for such a long time I'm humiliated," Mitchell said. "Your better half was consistently a fine good example for me when I was an adolescent, and I've generally respected him to such an extent. But I'm puzzled that of all people, I'd be one of three people he wants to see."

"I'm simply the courier, letting you know what my better half

mentioned." "Who are the other two?"

"He likewise needs Johnny Corleone and Josh Goldman to come in."

"My gosh, I haven't seen Johnny since my graduation. I read about him in all the business distributions. Did he say he'd come?"

"Yes. This Friday, and he's flying in from Boston."

"And Josh Goldman. I purchased my first suit that was definitely not a rummage at his dad's men's shop. Josh was that thin child who kicked those three field objectives against Jacktown. What's he up to these days?"

"He's a secondary teacher in Dayton. I passed on a message on his machine to call me. Will you come, Mitch, and provided that this is true, be here by early afternoon? I'll eat waiting."

"Indeed, ma'am. I'll be there. You and Coach Morris actually live in a similar house down from the school?"

"No, we're on North Market Street now."

"No chance, Mrs. M. Try not to let me know you and Coach live in one of those old Victorian houses we as a whole called Mansion Row? I'm dazzled. Seems as though Coach did approve selling genuine estate."

"He's progressed admirably, Johnny. Back in the mid '80s, those huge houses were selling at unequaled lows. They couldn't part with them. That is when Coach purchased the Miller chateau at 800 North Market."

"The Miller house! I realize it well. Henry Miller was a bigwig at River

Steel, way back when, right? Then the Gibson family bought it, and I used to shovel their snow. Furthermore one summer, I helped my dad paint it. Sure brings back old recollections. Is that green gazebo still in the patio? I recollect when it was red, however Mrs. Gibson needed it painted green, so I painted it for her."

"It's still there yet presently it's red once more," Mrs. Morris replied. "Mentor and I figured it ought to be red."

"Indeed, I'll come, ma'am."

Her voice broke again as she said, "Many thanks, Mitch. My significant other and I anticipate seeing you on Friday."

"SaMe here, Mrs. M."

It was almost 7:00 when Josh Goldman returned home. At 5'8", the trim teacher had a full head of wavy dull hair. With his innocent looks and excellent of humor, he was very well known with his students.

"Sorry I'm late, honey," he said to his better half, Sarah, "however the soccer practice went longer than typical. Where are the kids?"

"I gave them their supper at six. Maggie's higher up contemplating, and Timmy has band practice."

"Definitely, I heard them playing during practice."

"I checked the replying Mail this evening when I returned home from work. There's an intriguing message on it for you. It's from Mrs. M. Who's she?"

"Well, let me think. Goodness no doubt, that would be Mrs. Morris. Jack Morris' better half. He's my old secondary school football trainer. I can't help thinking about what she needs. I'll call her right now."

"Would you mind talking to her later, honey? Right now we should talk about braces for Maggie." Sarah moaned, removing food from the cooler. "I conversed with Dr. Sharp today who said Maggie needs them now. Furthermore supports cost a fortune. I've been pondering how we can bear the cost of it, and I've chosen to work the 12 PM shift at the medical clinic. The compensation is four dollars an hour higher."

"In no way, shape or form," Josh embedded. "No 12 PM shift. I'll sort out another method for enhancing my instructing salary."

"Like what?"

"I'll quit training soccer and work every summer. I'll moonlight during the school year. I can paint houses throughout the mid year. I'll sell Amway. I can sell genuine estate."

"I prefer not to come down on you, darling," Sarah said delicately. "What's more you realize how economical I am. If we didn't need the money, I wouldn't even bring the subject up. It's simply that the orthodontist is discussing eight thousand

dollars."

"8,000 dollars!" Josh shouted. "Abruptly, I appear to have lost my appetite."

Looking at the stressed demeanor on his significant other's face, he said in a quiet voice, "Relax, honey. We'll figure out how to sort out things. We generally do."

"I know, Josh. In any case, it appears to be that regardless of how hard we work and save, something consistently comes up and clears out what little we have in the bank."

On October 1, 2003, Josh Goldman went home for the day from his encouraging position to visit his old football trainer in Lincoln, Ohio. Since Dayton was close to the Indiana boundary and Lincoln near Pennsylvania, it was almost a four-hour drive across Buckeye Land. Josh topped off the tank of his Honda Accord, computing that he could come to Lincoln and mostly back home on a full tank. Typically he generally preferred not to drive such a significant distance alone, however it was a brilliant, clear pre-winter day and he anticipated survey the ravishing fall tones. In the event that he needed to pick a season to pass through his home express, this would be it, when he thought Ohio was generally lovely. He was additionally restless to visit Lincoln. He had just been there once since his family moved to the Cleveland region in 1977, and that was for his 10th secondary school gathering. The gathering was a setback on the grounds that the town was significantly more discouraged than Josh had recollected. The vast majority of his cohorts had moved away, and less than half went to the gathering. "It was simply too early," an old schoolmate remarked, "on the grounds that no one had done anything adequately huge to have procured gloating rights."

During his excursion, Josh contemplated experiencing childhood in Lincoln. What he recollected for the most part about his secondary school days was his father's steady condition of misery—by the last part of the '60s Goldman's Clothiers was scarcely equaling the initial investment. As a young fellow, his dad, Harry Goldman, had moved to Ohio from the Bronx. He traveled west in 1951 to address the Doubleday Shirt Company. Initially, Harry resided in Cleveland where he met Libby Marks. They were hitched in 1954, and after three years she bore him a child whom they named Joshua, which they thought was a delightful scriptural name. After the birth, she inquired as to whether it would be feasible to consider another line

of work, whatever didn't need being out and about. "In case a decent chance comes my direction," he guaranteed her, "I'll truly consider it."

In 1958, Robert Churchill, the proprietor of Churchill's Haberdashery, Lincoln's driving men's store, declared that he planned to resign. This was the chance that Harry Goldman was hanging tight for. Churchill's was one of Harry's records, and he thought of it as one of the most outstanding dealt with men's stores in his region. He was likewise very attached to Mr. Churchill, a superb trader and a man of high integrity.

When Harry Goldman talked to Churchill about purchasing his business, there were no other interested parties. "Shortly after the steel company shut down," Harry Goldman had told his son, "Mr. Churchill was planning to close the store's doors, so he was thrilled to have a buyer. I had very little money, so I made him an offer with only a small down payment. I signed a ten-year note, and Mr. Churchill accepted my offer in a heartbeat." Shortly after the sale, Mr. Churchill moved to Naples, Florida, and for the next ten years received a monthly check from Harry Goldman.

While Churchill's had a strong standing, Harry Goldman changed the name to Goldman's. "Churchill was such a WASP name," Josh reviews his dad telling him. "I didn't need individuals to feel that a Jew would pick a British-sounding name for dread they would think I was attempting to conceal my Jewish character." Reminiscing about his dad's thinking made him laugh. In Josh's eyes, his dad's appearance and thick New York complement were the exemplification of the generalized Jew. Regardless of whether Harry Goldman had changed his last name to Churchill, his Jewishness would remain completely intact.

Josh recollected his dad letting him know that the store would sometime be his. But having witnessed how his father struggled to make ends meet, Josh wanted no part of it. Josh shook his head to shake off the recollections and murmured. Interesting how contemplating his dad's monetary battles helped him to remember his own. Coming up with eight thousand for the orthodontist was a frightening thought. It would not just crash the family's investment account, it would place them under water. He quickly reflected about having Maggie do without supports. For a couple of brief seconds, an idea hustled through his brain of the large numbers of youngsters all around the world that get by without having their teeth fixed, and they figure out how to make due. Then he felt ashamed for having such a notion. Maggie will have supports, Josh guaranteed himself.

Most of the way to Lincoln and simply past Zanesville, Ohio, Josh Goldman's
contemplations floated to Coach Morris and his days as the Lions' kicker. Josh never dominated in sports. He just played football his lesser and senior years, and as a kicker, he never distinguished himself as an athlete. With a solitary exemption, his physicality couldn't ever have been recalled by anybody, himself included. That special case was his three field objectives in the Lincoln-Jacktown game on November 7, 1975. His presentation on that noteworthy evening was absolutely the feature of his athletic profession; nothing in life previously or since had verged on matching the high he had felt that evening. He had remembered his presentation multiple times since, regularly when he was down. During low periods, the memory of that evening quite often helped his soul. It gave him certainty that he could do whatever he put a lot of focus on doing.

YOU CAN DO WHATEVER YOU
SET YOUR MIND ON DOING.

Josh had another common idea—one not exactly as clear as envisioning those three astonishing field objectives sail past the goal line and the relating cheers from the group. Also that was what he encountered the prior night. The Pep Talk. At that point, The Pep Talk scarcely bothered him. But over the years, he remembered bits and pieces of it, and in time, perhaps even the entire pep talk. *How abnormal*, he thought, since he was unable to try and review the man's name who gave it. Nor had he at any point examined it with any other individual. Furthermore at that point, in light of the fact that The Pep Talk was Christian-skewed, he felt that it wasn't intended to be aimed at him, the main Jewish player on the 1975 Lincoln crew. All things considered, in his sub-conscience, he subliminally realized that it some way or another impacted his life. If not, for what reason could he ceaselessly harp on it? For what reason would he review portions of it word for word? For what reason would he return to it in his fantasies throughout a fourth of a century?

It required somewhat more than three hours from the time Johnny Corleone left his rich apartment on Nob Hill, Boston's most world class address, got into a limousine, loaded up the organization Gulf Stream, and showed up at a little air terminal close to Youngstown, Ohio, only 35 miles due north of Lincoln, Ohio. After arriving in Ohio, a gleaming Lincoln Continental was holding up for

him, a simple twenty yards from where the stream had halted. Corleone collapsed the guide he had considered during his trip to retain the headings, including a couple dirt roads he reviewed from his childhood that didn't show up on the map.

"I'll call your wireless when I'm prepared to leave Lincoln this evening," he told his two pilots. You have my cell number, right Jack?"
"Yes sir, chief. Partake in the ride. You sure got an all around flawless day for it.
And drive safely."

Once in the driver's seat, Johnny loose and partook in the ride. As he got closer to Lincoln, he perceived some old destinations he hadn't seen for such countless years. He thought about his childhood, and how his father hopped from job to job, always searching for work that would pay high wages like what he earned back in the '50s when he was a foreman in the steel mill. Those were prosperous years before Johnny was conceived, the ones his father consistently alluded to as "old fashioned days."

It wasn't until years after the family had moved to Toledo that his dad again got a nice manufacturing plant work at the Jeep plant. Every one of Johnny's family members were steady common laborers who had at some time worked in either steel factories or coal mines.

Johnny Corleone was one of the untouched most well known children at Lincoln High School. He was gorgeous, a researcher competitor, and simply a truly decent child. He was a preferred researcher over a competitor—recall now, the Lions had their most exceedingly awful at any point record during his rudder as the Lions' quarterback. Be that as it may, Lincoln was a workingman's town, so except for a couple of individuals from the school personnel, no one truly gave a lot of consideration to his scholastic accomplishments. Regardless of anything else, Johnny was a fantastic pioneer. As a grown-up, he now and again ascribed his initiative abilities to the time he spent quarterbacking an awful football crew. "Talking about affliction, I adapted extensively more with regards to initiative by playing in a losing group," he was attached to saying at the executives courses when making reference to his secondary school football days.

Johnny likewise often cited Ernest Hemingway's Farewell to Arms when he talked about misfortune. "The world breaks everybody, and subsequently many are more grounded at the messed up places," he regularly told youthful bank employees.

WHen his bike mishap finished his football vocation, he accepted it. Johnny realized he had no future in football after secondary school.   He considered the group's helpless record as generally a humiliation, yet nothing he was embarrassed about. All things considered, football was just a game. He appreciated playing it, and specifically he adored the fellowship. Win or lose, he was a cooperative person, a quality that served him well all through his career.

There was as a general rule just a solitary time when he dominated on the football field. Also that was the night he finished twenty out of 28 passes against Jacktown. The Game. He always remembered the fervor of that game. How well he recalled the adrenalin that shot through his whole body! The fervor of the group. The fulfillment of realizing he was in charge of his fate. The holding he felt that evening with his partners. The trust he had in them, realizing that each play depended on the execution of each individual from the crew taking care of his business. Also obviously the trust they had in him. It was a collaboration. In many cases a short time later, Johnny would re-make the game to him. He particularly partook in the thrill he felt realizing that when he flung the football, it was bound to show up at its definite objective. That evening, maybe he was delivering directed rockets as opposed to tossing passes. He knew each pass he tossed would track down its planned recipient. It didn't make any difference that the objective was a moving objective. Every one of the pieces had fallen together during that mystical game, and it was a rush that Johnny will always remember. Nor did he at any point need to neglect. To this end he ceaselessly played mental reruns of The Game. Furthermore each time he did, he'd get a high.

It was weird how that one game had deleted all of the booing that JGoodnessnny and his partners suffered during their long losing streak. Those misfortunes. A large number of games after game. For some time, maybe the group could always lose once more. Also when it came time to play his last football match-up ever against Jacktown, no one around allowed them an opportunity over the strong Giants. Indeed, a large portion of his football recollections were about dissatisfactions. But the only one that really mattered to Johnny Corleone was the way their team performed in The Game. Oh, and something different entered his thoughts as he traveled down the country roads: The Pep Talk that was given to the group the prior night. Johnny had always remembered it. It was given by a Mr. What's-his-name?

For a really long time Johnny had thought hard attempting to recall who it was that gave that motivational speech. It was amusing that he was unable to recall the more abnormal's name, however he was positive that the man wore a fedora with a red quill in the hatband. Johnny couldn't imagine what he resembled by any means, aside from the cap he wore. Much odder was the way that he recollected the man's message

exhaustively. He heard Joshua 1:9, a sacred writing that he since much of the time cited: "Be solid and gallant; don't be terrified or overwhelmed for the LORD your God is with you any place you go." Johnny had rehashed these words to himself just as to others commonly. In particular, this sacred text had helped him through troublesome occasions throughout his life.

Johnny likewise asked an incredible arrangement, and he wasn't modest with regards to let individuals know that he asked—he even discussed supplication at conferences. It didn't make any difference who was available, he every now and again cited Mark 11:24: "Whatever you request in petition, accept that you have gotten it, and it will be yours." Afterward, he was inclined to add, "I know since I have supplicated and I have received."

Mark Mitchell drove a major dark Mercedes to Lincoln. He left not long before 9:00 a.m., despite the fact that it was just a more than two hour ride from Columbus. It had been a long while since his last visit to Lincoln, and once out and about, as Josh and Johnny, he likewise started to ponder what it resembled experiencing childhood in a modest community thirty years prior; it appeared to be light years from his life now. After he moved on from secondary school, he was a page in the Ohio Senate during school, because of Irwin Benson, a state congressperson from Lincoln who made some things happen to get him the work. In the summers, he had painted houses with his father.

"I need you to have a well-rounded schooling and make a big deal about yourself," Mark recalled his dad more than once telling him as they worked. "I don't need you to go through your time on earth painting houses like your dad. You're better compared to that."

Thinking about his dad leaving Imprint's eyes water, and tears began running down his cheeks. It had been a very long time since he had cried, and he thought that it is to some degree humiliating. Actually no, not humiliating, more like lowering. He wanted that his dad was alive to partake in his prosperity at the bank. He would have been so glad. Mark had consistently flourished with causing his dad to feel proud.

Mark recollected how pleased his dad was the point at which he turned into the beginning linebacker for the Lincoln Lions. He additionally reviewed his dad telling him not to

be debilitate during the group's long, long losing streak. As he headed to Lincoln, Mark roared with laughter when he contemplated his dad's cheesy saying: "It's not the canine in the battle that matters. It's the battle in the canine that matters." And as cliché as he observed the statement, he frequently utilized a similar line when addressing bank employees.

Most of the way to Lincoln, his considerations floated to The Pep Talk. Like Johnny and Josh, he had additionally mulled over everything throughout the long term, and like they, he recollected pieces and bits of parts; some he brought up word for word. He started contemplating The Game, and specifically, how he played at a level that he never imagined he was equipped for playing. *I was wherever on the field that evening*, Mark recalled. *I played my heart out on the grounds that I would have rather not let my partners down. I just weighed 165 pounds, and I was making hits against Jacktown players twice my size. I was fearless.*

Although he never again had an encore on the football field that came anyplace near how he played in the major event, the information that he had dominated had given him certainty to take a stab at more yearning objectives later in his life. He accepted that the sky is the limit, regardless of how extraordinary the chances are. "I can achieve anything that I put a lot of focus on. 'Favored are the people who have not seen but have come to accept,'" he said without holding back. "John 20:29." Throughout his life, those words had served him well.

THE REUNION

Having the shortest distance to travel, Mark was the first to arrive in Lincoln. Once inside the city limits, he passed by the big steel mill on the south side of town. It was still there, a shadow of its former self. Fifty years later, the mill remained unoccupied—all three million square feet of it, an eyesore of nearly seventy acres. The humongous dark construction was rusted; each window was broken and barricaded. Its gigantic smoke stacks appeared to droop and hang over. Weeds and trees had developed through its asphalted parking garage. A chain fence finished off with spiked metal encompassed it with large, striking signs cautioning intruders to remain away or be prosecuted.

Once past the modern part of town, Mark drove down Main Street through the midtown region just because. Just halting for one of the three traffic signals in the six-block business segment, he shrouded Lincoln's fundamental avenue in under forty seconds. Downtown Lincoln seemed to be like how he recollected that it. However, the three pharmacies had been supplanted by a Wendy's, a Subway, and a pre-owned book shop. What's more there was not any more Goldman's. It was a blocked retail facade. One of his own State National Bank offices involved the corner part that had once been a Gulf Oil Station. Another sight that would have satisfied his dad.

Mark took a left turn on North Market, and a couple of squares from the business region stood those grand Victorian homes that he respected as a kid. He was amazed that these impressive homes were pretty much as large as he recalled. *These respectable homes have withstood everyday hardship*, he thought to himself.

Spotting the 800 North Market Street address, Mark promptly perceived the old Miller Mansion, probably the greatest house in the region. The house was worked in 1912. Mark stopped close to the control and strolled up the driveway.

Margaret Morris welcomed him at the entryway. "You're . .

." "Mitch," he replied. "Mrs. M., you haven't changed at all."

"You positively have," she answered. "Obviously, you were only a kid when I last saw you. Presently take a gander at you. You look taller than I recalled, and you've added a couple pounds."

"I was just seventeen when I graduated Lincoln, and you're correct ma'am. I became another two creeps in my first year at OSU, and today I'm twenty pounds heavier. Had I had one more year in secondary school, I may have been a superior football player for Coach."

"Mentor and I have followed your profession," she said. "Who might have at any point envisioned you'd be a hotshot financier?" Changing the subject she said, "My significant other is in the library. This is whenever this week first he's been out of the room. Thank the Lord, Coach is having a decent day. I'm certain knowing you three would be here today has helped his spirits. Come on, how about we go see him."

"One of your young men is here," she reported, making the way for the library. Jack Morris was in his night robe, wearing a naval force shower robe, and sitting in a cowhide seat behind his desk.

Mark didn't show it when he went into the room, however had the fact of the matter been known, he would not have perceived his previous football trainer. Morris was a shell of the strong man Mark recalled. He looked impressively more established than his seventy or more years.

"Incredible to see you, Coach. You haven't transformed one bit throughout the long term." "All things considered, you sure have, Mitch," Morris said in a frail voice. "For the better, I may add."

"A significant cushion you have here, Coach. I take it the land business concurs with you."

"I've done approve," Morris answered. "I applied a similar stuff I showed you folks in football—it works in business too."

"Like what?"

"first off, discipline," Coach said. "You must be a self-starter to sell land because you're your own chief. You go back and forth however you see fit. No proper hours. Then too, you've got to be prepared. You should get your work done before you show a property—here most land individuals are frail. By getting my work done, I generally felt as though I had an edge on the opposition. Furthermore like most organizations, it's tied in with building associations with individuals. Uh oh, sorry, Mitch, however you got me started."

"No, no. I hear you, Coach. Seems like the very rules that work in the banking business.

"Driving up Market Street, I saw how all around kept up with these Victorian homes are," Mark said. "With the discouraged financial conditions in Lincoln, I thought they'd room houses and changed over into low-end apartments."

"It involved community pride," Morris said. "As a real estate agent, I headed a mission to save these houses. Ensured the drafting laws kept them from deteriorating."

Twenty minutes after the fact Josh Goldman strolled in the entryway, and not long before early afternoon, Johnny Corleone showed up. "All present and represented," Morris said. After the four men had become reacquainted, at 12:30 Margaret Morris got a plate with soup and sandwiches. She left the room and got back with a plate of potato chips, natively constructed treats, and delicate drinks.

"So Coach, you didn't do not good enough for yourself," Johnny said, checking out the mentor's open study.

"Those land commissions sure beat an instructor's compensation, didn't they, Coach?" Josh said.

"Valid," Morris remarked, "yet they never verged on giving me the work fulfillment that came from working with youthful people.

"When you get to the phase of life where I am," he added, "the measure of cash you've aggregated isn't what makes a difference. It's how you've helped others."

IT'S NOT ABOUT THE AMOUNT OF MONEY YOU'VE ACCUMULATED, BUT WHAT YOU'VE DONE FOR OTHERS.

"I'm with you on that," Johnny said, and Mark nodded.

"It's simple for both of you to say," Josh prodded. "You folks are zillionaires. What's Alpha's stock exchanging at nowadays, Johnny? I read that each time it goes up a point, you make another couple of million. Also Mark, what amount are your State National investment opportunities worth these days?"

"Every one of you three have been exceptionally effective in your profession," Jack Morris interrupted. "I'm similarly glad for every one of you. Say, did both of you know

that last April, Josh was named Ohio Teacher of the Year?"

"No, yet that is a significant honor," Johnny said.

"Congrats," Mark said, tapping his companion on the back.

"Folks, there is soMething I need to converse with you three about," Morris broke in. "It's something been at the forefront of my thoughts for quite a while. I know Mrs. M. has informed you regarding my growth and that I'm at death's doorstep. Indeed, truly, folks, I welcomed you three here in light of the fact that I want a few answers that you could very well have for me before I settle up with here . . ." The elderly person's voice broke, and he halted in his sentence.

"I was asking why you asked us," Mark said, breaking the respite in the discussion. "Assuming that it were simply me and Johnny, I'd think it was a result of our attractive features. However at that point Josh is here so that is governed out."

Nobody giggled. It was anything but a period for levity.

"You have us fascinated, Coach. What's happening?"

Johnny inquired. "Furthermore why us?" Josh added.

"Presently where do I start?" Jack Morris said with a slight faltering. "How about we return to what has been alluded to as 'The Game.' The night we beat Jacktown."

"When individuals hear I'm from Lincoln," Josh interposed, "the primary thing they ask is, 'Were you at The Game?' I've had outsiders let me know that the Lincoln kicker had three field objectives, all from in excess of 50 yards out."

"Simply last week, there was an article in the Columbus Dispatch that referenced The Game," Mark smiled. "For quite a long time, they've been contrasting bombshells of significant Ohio groups with the Lincoln-Jacktown game."

"I didn't assume any of you would fail to remember that game," Coach Morris said, "however what I truly need to know is this: Do any of you recollect that anything about The Pep Talk the night prior to the game?"

At the accompanying quietness, a look of disillusionment showed up all over. "I thought without a doubt that one of you . . ." Morris began to say. "Doesn't it ring a bell? Do any of you . . ."

"Indeed, I recollect it well overall," Corleone chipped in. Then, at that point, Mark and Goldman gestured their heads affirming that they likewise recollected it.

"Does anybody want to expound?" Morris asked.

At first no one chipped in. Following a couple of seconds of quietness, Mark

unobtrusively said, "OK. I've pondered it significantly throughout the long term. Without a doubt, I admit that I consider it frequently. In actuality, only today, on my drive here from Columbus, I was pondering it."

"Strangely, me as well," Josh said sheepishly.

"Do you mean you consider it like Mitch?" Johnny inquired, "or you coincidentally thought about it in transit here today?"

"Both. Maybe I've never quit thinking about that motivational speech. Furthermore like Mitch, coming here today, I pictured myself staying there in the storage space that evening, paying attention to that outsider with the extravagant cap. Meanwhile, I was taking in all that the man said."

Getting up out of his seat, Corleone said, "This discussion is giving me goose pimples. Allow me to let you know something that I've never told anybody, not even my better half. I can recall such a great deal what that man let us know that evening that it's tremendously shocking. The truth of the matter is, I can't start to stop for a minute an impact it's had on my life. You've all found out about something happening to an individual that he alludes to as a pivotal occasion in his life. I accept that is the manner by which The Pep Talk impacted me."

"I can't start to communicate how much hearing you say that means to me," Morris intruded, all over lighting up.

"How's that, Coach?" Corleone asked.

"It's lastingly affected me as well. Be that as it may, I've conversed with a significant number of different players in the course of the most recent couple of years, and no one, and I mean no one, had even a dubious memory about The Pep Talk. Some said they figured I may have said something to the group that got them started up, yet that is it. No one recalls Mr. Christopher."

"Christopher, that is his name!" Corleone shouted. "I was unable to recall his name to save my life."

"Nor could I," said Goldman, "yet I have an unclear memory concerning what he resembled. Nonetheless, I wouldn't need the obligation of recognizing him in a police setup. Except if obviously he was the just one wearing a tweed cap with a red plume in the hatband."

"Right," Johnny tolled in, "the man wore a fedora, and indeed, it had a red quill. Helped me to remember Bear Bryant. I'm alluding to the cap, not Mr. Christopher. Odd, how you recollect a little detail like that, isn't it?"

"You should, 'Mitch?" Coach asked.

"I don't know I could possibly do get his name, but rather I positively recall him, and indeed, the cap," Mark said. "Inform us concerning him, Coach. Who was he?"

"Very little to tell," Morris replied. "Early that morning, I met the man at Abe's Lincoln Diner. He presented himself and went along with me for some espresso. Said he was an outsider around. I figured he was a sales rep going through. We got to chatting casually and before I knew it, he said he might want to give a motivational speech to the group and I affirmed it. Presently for the existence of me, I was unable to explain to you why I agreed to let a more peculiar give a discussion to the group, especially a man who was just thirty-something. Nevertheless, there was something I preferred with regards to him. He was so genuine and he had a decent, lovely way."

"He was just thirty?" Mark said. "He appeared to be more established. Obviously when you're seventeen, anybody north of 25 is ancient."

"What might be said about after The Pep Talk? Josh inquired. "What did you talk about with him?"

"Before I could express gratitude toward him, he was gone. Never saw him again. Truly, at the time I wasn't even certain that what he said implied anything to any of you guys."

"No doubt, I recollect there was a break in the room after he got done," Mark said. "No mix at all. Just silence."

"Maybe the group couldn't figure out his message," Josh said.

"It wasn't the sort of motivational speech you hope to hear in storage spaces," Johnny said. "It was more similar to something you'd hear in chapel. But that's not quite it either. I recollect how he cited the Bhagavad Gita. I don't consider any us had at any point known about it in those days. I didn't have the foggiest idea what the Bhagavad Gita was until my senior year in school when a teacher discussed dharma during a talk on Eastern way of thinking. Like I say, a great deal of what this Mr. Christopher said presumably flew right by us, henceforth the quiet response when he finished."

"A few weeks later, I was still thinking about his pep talk," Morris interjected. "I wanted to talk to him about it. I wanted to thank him, so I started to do some inquiring. Now, remember there was no Internet—I couldn't go online to do a search on him. Mr. Christopher said he was originally from Bethlehem, a steel town in Eastern Pennsylvania with a big reputation in sports for its great athletes. I called all of the high school football coaches in the Lehigh Valley, but nobody ever heard hide nor hair of him. I even mentioned the fedora. I remembered that Mr. Christopher said he grew up in the area and had moved to Philadelphia. I never did know his first name, and Philadelphia is too big a city to find a 'Mr. Christopher,' so I gave up trying to find him. However, every now and then I'd meet someone from Philly, and when I did, I'd describe our Mr. Christopher and what I knew about him. But nobody ever knew anyone that fit his description."

"Anybody in Lincoln know at least something about him? You said he was passing through. Assuming he was in the cafe at 6:00 a.m., he probably remained some place close by," Mark questioned.

"Very savvy, Mitch," Morris said, "and I called the River Hotel and every one of the inns nearby. Once more, I struck out."

"What might be said about the server? Did she know at least something about him?"

"That was Beatrice. She was the just one in the burger joint during the time Mr. Christopher and I were there," Morris said. "She said, 'I just enigmatically recollect you conversing with somebody, however what do I know? Such countless clients going as the week progressed. They come and they go.' She was dumbfounded. She was unable to try and recall his fedora.

"Not having the option to observe him truly got to me," Morris proceeded. "Occasionally, I'd stroll down the road, or at a public spot like an Ohio State football match-up, and I'd spot a person wearing a fedora. So I was continually being helped to remember him. At least a few times, I'd see a man wearing a fedora strolling with his back toward me, and I'd hurry to stretch out beyond him to check whether he was Mr. Christopher. Like I said, it truly got to me."

"For what reason was it so significant for you to converse with him, Coach?" Johnny asked.

"I can't genuinely address that inquiry, Johnny," Morris moaned and shrugged his shoulders. "I assume there was only something about him that got to me. You know, how we played the round of our lives against Jacktown. Truth be told, it was absolutely impossible that I figured we could beat them. They were far unrivaled competitors in each position. Furthermore all around trained. Jacktown's lead trainer, Rich Hart, later instructed at Texas Southern.

"After I resigned as lead trainer and began selling land full-time, I reflected with regards to the Jacktown game. I continued to ask myself what we did to dominate that match. Maybe a heavenly messenger was looking after us. We couldn't be blamed under any circumstance . . . Josh making those three field objectives. With all due regard Josh, you never hit one from 34 yards out before that game.   Johnny

contended twenty for 29 and ran the ball grandly. What's more you, Mitch, 24 handles. Come on folks. You were all playing such a long ways over your heads—and against Jacktown.

"All things considered, I began mulling over everything, and the main thing I could figure that was unique in relation to our different games was The Pep Talk. But I couldn't make any sense out of it. One thing the four of us do know—it was no customary motivational speech. See how it's left with every one of all of your lives. Would you be able to recall that anything about some other motivational speech you at any point heard? You've heard me give them at rehearses, before games, at halftimes."

"Not actually, Coach," Josh said. "I can't sincerely recollect one of yours other than the way that you gave them. It was simply such a long time ago, Coach. But what I can't get over is how well I do remember Mr.

Christopher's energy talk."

"OK, so we as a whole recall it," Johnny said. "There are bunches of things we hear when we're kids that stay with us. Especially when we're youthful and impressionable."

BELIEVE IN YOURSELF.

"Really," Mark embedded, "I do recall one motivational speech you put forth a strong effort. The one I'm alluding to was at halftime during The Game."

"Gracious indeed, and it was a decent one," Johnny said. "I recall it as well. You let us know that the Jacktown Giants were not goliaths all things considered, and you advised us that we had kept it together with them for the main half, and that if we would do it for the initial two quarters, we could do it for the following two. You caused us to put stock in ourselves."

"Indeed, I recollect that one as well," Josh added. "You told us not to zero in on the scoreboard and to execute our singular task—each play in turn. What's more trust. You underlined trust. Trust every one of our colleagues to tackle his task. Indeed, and you told the linemen to 'dominate the container,' and you said we should simply continue to establish grass. You said a great deal of the things that Mr. Christopher had told us during The Pep Talk."

"You likewise cited Mark 11:24: 'Whatever you request in petition, accept that you have gotten it, and it will be yours,'" Johnny said. Furthermore you requested that we say a petition before the beginning of the subsequent half. You're correct, Mitch, that was Coach's best ever motivational speech. You truly had us started up for the second
half."

"A debt of gratitude is in order for the demonstration of positive support," Morris said. "Presently I have something to show you, and this will knock your socks off. I've assembled a scrapbook. When you see it, I think you'll comprehend the reason why I needed you here today."

THE SCRAPBOOK

J ack Morris slowly walked across the spacious room to retrieve a large scrapbook from the bookshelf on the far side of the study.

"You're holding that like it's the Holy Grail," Johnny remarked.

"All around put," Morris replied, putting the huge scrapbook on the work area. "It might just be the Holy Grail.'"

"half a month prior, Margaret brought down from the loft this large number of old boxes containing photographs and news clippings," Morris said, highlighting the opposite side of the room. "She figured it would be great treatment for me to go through them. I obliged her, for the most part to pacify her. But she was right. The old recollections ended up being remedial. They took my brain off my ailment. I don't have the foggiest idea why however I began to classify everything sequentially," Morris kept, flipping through pages of the scrapbook. "This is the point at which I ran over these old news clippings about the Jacktown game.

"Disregard the wide range of various stuff," Morris kept, highlighting the opened scrapbook. "I need you to take a gander at the articles on these pages. Beginning here with the part about the Jacktown game. Here's the place where it begins to get truly interesting."

His three visitors remained behind him, investigating his shoulder. "Give close consideration to these articles specifically," Morris instructed.

The features read:

MARK MITCHELL BREAKS UP 11 PASSES,
HAS 24 TACKLES

JOHNNY CORLEONE COMPLETES 20 OUT OF 29

KICKER JOSH GOLDMAN, NUMBER 1,
OUTSCORES JACKTOWN WITH 9

"I recollect those articles," Josh said.

Morris took out Xeroxed duplicates of the three articles and with a yellow feature pen, he said, "Presently watch carefully."

In the principal article, he featured MARK, 11, and

24. In the second article he featured JOHN, 20, and

29.

In the third article he featured JOSH, 1, and 9. After the word JOSH, he added the letters UA.

"Have any of you sorted out what I've done?" he asked.

Nobody said a word. "Look what we arrived," he said as he composed on a legitimate cushion in huge, strong letters:

MARK 11:24.

JOHN 20:29

JOSHUA 1:9

"Presently do you get it?"

"Book of scriptures sections," Josh said. "However, what's it mean?"

"Before I clarify, let me quote sacred text to you," Coach Morris proceeded. "Mark 11:24 peruses, 'Whatever you request in petition, accept that you have gotten it, and it will be yours.'"

"I can take it from here, Coach," Johnny said. "John 20:29 peruses, 'Favored are the individuals who have not seen but then have come to accept.'" Then he added, "'Be solid and bold; don't be scared or disheartened, for the LORD your God is with you any place you go.' That's Joshua 1:9."

"You know your Bible well," Mitch said. "I'm impressed."

"I'm not as good as you think," Johnny answered. "I happen to know those three passages because they were the scriptures that Mr. Christopher quoted in his pep talk. Somehow, deep in here somewhere," he continued, placing his index finger to his head, "Mr. Christopher's words got to me. I can't quote much from the Bible, but I do know those scriptures."

"Were there some other sacred writings spoken by Mr. Christopher?"

Mark inquired. "Indeed, one more," Morris answered.

"Truth be told," Mitch chipped in. "He cited one of my beloved sections, which is John 15:12. It's the place where Christ says, 'This is my charge, that you love each other as I have adored you.' Any articles make reference to this one?"

"No, Mitch. None that I've gone over," Morris answered.

"So what's this all mean?" Josh asked.

"That is the reason I requested that all of you come," Morris said. "It's been at the forefront of my thoughts since the time I began assembling this scrapbook, however I don't know what to think about it.

"One thing I do know," he added. "I sure don't have any desire to lie on my deathbed never knowing the appropriate response. Furthermore the manner in which things stand presently, that is an unmistakable possibility."

Nobody said a word. Then Johnny spoke, carefully choosing his words. "I'm verbally processing on this one, people. Presently hold on for me. Here are current realities as we probably are aware them. Number one: This Mr.

Christopher appeared suddenly. He was an outright more interesting who gave a motivational speech that we all heard ages ago, but then the four of us here in this room plainly recollect portions of maybe it were yesterday."

"Two: According to Coach, none of different folks who were there appear to review The Pep Talk," Mark added.

"And three: We three players are the only ones concerning whom there is comparing sacred writing," Josh said, "and most perplexing is the way that this Mr. Christopher utilized these references before the game."

"Precisely," Morris intruded on, "sacred writing that coordinated your names with your exhibitions in the game, and for your situation Josh, your shirt number and your nine focuses. Consider it, young men. What can it mean?"

The room was indeed extremely peaceful. At last, Josh ended the quiet. "Assuming I may, I request your consent to assume the part of villain's advocate."

"Definitely," Mark said.

"I as of late had a conversation with my 11th grade history understudies," Josh said, "that I believe is pertinent to what in particular has occurred here. I'm certain you've found out about the well known Abraham Lincoln and John Kennedy happenstances, however kindly hold on for me and permit me to get done so I can make my point.

"Lincoln was chosen for Congress in 1846. Kennedy was chosen for Congress in 1946. Lincoln was chosen president in 1860, Kennedy in 1960. The names Lincoln and Kennedy each contain seven letters. The two spouses lost their youngsters while residing in the White House. The two presidents were shot on a Friday, and both in the head."

"I'm familiar with what you're saying," Mark said. "Both were killed by Southerners, and both were prevailed by Southerners. The two replacements were named Johnson."

"Awesome, Mitch," Johnny said. "That would be Andrew Johnson, who succeeded Lincoln and was brought into the world in 1808, and Lyndon Johnson, who succeeded Kennedy and was brought into the world in 1908. I likewise recall perusing that John Wilkes Booth, who killed Lincoln, was brought into the world in 1839 and Lee Harvey Oswald who shot Kennedy was brought into the world in 1939."

"You got it," Josh interfered, "and the two professional killers were known by their three names, and each had a name with fifteen letters. Corner ran from a theater and was trapped in a stockroom while Oswald ran from a distribution center and was trapped in a theater. Lincoln was taken shots at the Ford Theater, and Kennedy was shot in a Lincoln vehicle, a Ford item. Furthermore Booth and Oswald were killed before their preliminaries. Did you realize that Lincoln's secretary was Ms. Kennedy and Kennedy's secretary was Ms. Lincoln?

"The message I provided for my group was that these were happenstances and that's it. For instance, I brought up to my understudies that the rundown just incorporates raw numbers that are happenstances yet the rundown avoids what are not. Lincoln was brought into the world in 1809 and Kennedy in 1917—on the off chance that a rundown is made out of the incidents it ought to likewise incorporate non-related statistical data points. For example, Lincoln had four children while Kennedy had a child and a girl. Lincoln's child was not killed in a plane accident, nor did Lincoln have a sibling who was head legal officer and was killed. I likewise let my understudies know that in case you will discuss the quantity of letters in their names, why not additionally notice that Booth's complete name has three letter o's when contrasted with one letter o for Oswald. Do you see where I'm going with this?"

"I guess I'm simply a withering elderly person who's getting a handle on for straws," Morris moaned. "Much obliged, Josh. What you just said makes a ton of sense."

Seeing the elderly person's mistake, Josh said, "Not really quick, Coach. Like I said, I was arguing just to argue, yet that doesn't mean I know what to think about this. What mind blowing chances that Mr. Christopher might have made reference to explicit sacred writings in The Pep Talk that would compare with the game details and afterward show up in those news clippings. Take a gander at those three title texts in the paper—and see what you've featured with our names matching our numbers and our exhibitions. Johnny finishing twenty out of 29 passes. Mark, a.k.a. Mitch, separating eleven passes and having 24 handles. And afterward there I am—Number 1 with

those three field objectives for nine points."

"Additionally consider the significant effect that The Pep Talk had on every one of our lives," Mark contributed. "How would you represent that? I agree with Josh's examinations among Lincoln and Kennedy. There are loads of incidents. Simply unadulterated occurrences. But I refuse to accept The Pep Talk and the consequences that occurred in The Game and the effects it had on our lives as coincidental."

"Then, at that point, what do you think about it?" Coach asked.

"It was God-enlivened," Mark said. "I accept it was God-propelled." "Like a marvel from scriptural occasions?" Josh questioned.

"Why not?" Johnny asked.

"You know, billions of individuals in this world implore God consistently," Mark said."We converse with Him in our supplications. We perceptibly express gratefulness to Him in chapel and at eating times. But if someone tells you that God talked to him, people say he's crazy. Indeed, I do accept God converses with us. We may not hear His voice, yet He imparts to us in alternate ways. He does it when He answers our supplications. He does it when He favors us. What's more I'm certain He does it when He outfits us with great considerations, gives us fortitude, and makes us indescribably pleased with affection. Noble men, permit me to cite John 20:29 by and by: 'Favored are the individuals who have not seen but have come to accept.' Is it important for God to show up in this room with the end goal for us to think of an unequivocal and intelligent clarification regarding what was the deal? Is that what we should have to have faith in God's work?"

"So be it, Brother Mitch," Josh said. "Well put."

"Young men, I am so thankful to you for visiting me today," Coach said. "I can't start to let you know how much this has intended to me."

"Representing Josh and Mitch," Johnny said, "it's implied such a great amount to us all, and we thank you."

"Approved," Josh and Mark said in unison.

"I'm totally worn out, young men, and need to sleep," Morris said. "Assuming one of you will help me to that couch over there."

"Would you be able to accept, it's almost four o'clock," Josh said, looking at his watch interestingly since they'd arrived.

The three men said their farewells to their old mentor and vowed to stay in contact with him. Margaret Morris came in with a cover and covered her

spouse who was presently laying serenely on the couch. She delicately kissed him on the temple and strolled her guests to the entryway. In the wake of trading embraces, her splitting words were, "It's implied such a great amount to Coach for you to be here today."

Walking to their vehicles, Mark said, "I figure the three of us ought to have a little visit before we head out in a different direction. What do you say we stop at Abe's Lincoln Diner for espresso? Do you have an additional a half hour to save, Johnny, before you get your plane?"

"My plane isn't going anyplace without me," Johnny said. "You should,

Josh?”

"We should do it.”

COFFEE AT THE DINER

A t 4:00 in the afternoon, a slow time of the day, the diner was empty. The diner's walls were covered with sports paraphernalia, most of which was devoted to the Lincoln Lions' football conquests of yesteryear.

"I figure we should find a spot at this table," Johnny proposed, highlighting a seat underneath an outlined article about The Game.

Seated at a corner toward the rear of the cafe, Johnny said, "Investigate this spot. Maybe we're in a time travel—all that's actually similar to I recollect it."

"I anticipate that old Abe should come walking out from the back any subsequent now," Mark said, and going to the server inquired, "We'd like some espresso, ma'am, and hello, does Abe Horowitz actually possess this place?”

"Who?"questioned the little youngster, negligent of the way that Abe Horowitz was the organizer and previous proprietor of where she worked.

"It doesn't matter, you just addressed my inquiry," Mark said.

When the server got back to the table with three espressos, highlighted the outlined article on the divider and said, "I bet everything and the kitchen sink in this town actually talk concerning that one. Is that right, ma'am?”

"It was played some time before I was conceived," she grinned, "yet indeed, they actually talk about it. My father was at the game, and each football season, I hear him discussing it with my uncles.”

After the server left, Mark said, "Presently that we're at this point not within the sight of Coach Morris, we can talk all the more uninhibitedly. I'm certain you both got the appearance of frustration all over when Josh began in with regards to the Lincoln/Kennedy incidents. I don't have the foggiest idea what precisely to make from the entire drivel, yet one thing I do know is that we should be mindful so as not to blast his air pocket. Assuming he has it to him that this is God-enlivened, so be it. How about we let him continue to

think it. There's nothing out of sorts about a man on his
deathbed being overcome with such thoughts."

"And are you certain that he's off-base?" Johnny asked.

"Not in the slightest degree," Mark replied. "However at that point there is consistently the likelihood that quite possibly he is. Furthermore at the danger of seeming like a Doubting Thomas, I'm of the assessment that the three of us ought to do all that we can to demonstrate or refute what Coach thinks. Presently don't misunderstand me, folks. Maybe I need conviction in the Scriptures. Remember, the Good Book tells us that faith is believing in the unseen, and for the record, I buy into that hook, line, and sinker. Having said that, I figure we should practice due persistence so we can sort out exactly what this is all about."

"I am sorry for raising that Lincoln/Kennedy relationship," Josh advertised. "It's simply my inclination to debate for the sake of debating, and at times I do it to my own disservice since I cast a sad remnant of an uncertainty on what I really accept. It should be the instructor in me. I end up testing current realities, never needing to acknowledge anything as it shows up on the surface."

"That is not all so terrible," Mark said. "We do exactly the same thing in business." "Am I perusing both of you right?" Johnny said mindfully. "I derive from
what I am hearing that you are both saying that perhaps Coach is on to
something. Be that as it may, before we discount this entire thing, we ought to all in all cooperate to find some substantial solutions. Am I in total agreement with you guys?"

"I will not represent Josh, however I accept this justifies digging into."

"I concur," Josh said. "Like we examined at Coach's, that motivational speech has been modified in my brain, and obviously in yours as well. This without help from anyone else warrants further exploration."

"That," considered Johnny, "in addition to the sacred writings thing. That is the thing that genuinely bewilders me. Indeed, there might be some coherent clarification, yet in case there is one, it sure has me stumped."

"We had a speaker at a retreat last year who recounted a superb story," Mark said. Presently it's genuinely long, yet it merits rehashing in light of the fact that its message is so fitting. It goes this way: There are four individuals on a train on the way from Paris to Barcelona—a lovely little youngster going with her older grandma, and an impressive general going with his helper, a youthful, attractive second lieutenant. The foursome is sitting peacefully as the train enters a passage in the Pyrenees, the mountain range on the line among France and Spain.

"It is black as night in the passage. Unexpectedly there's a boisterous kiss, trailed by a subsequent sound, that of an uproarious, hard smack. After leaving the passage, the four individuals stay quiet, with nobody recognizing the incident.

"The little kid ponders internally, *Boy, that was a swell kiss that attractive lieutenant gave me, and I truly appreciated it. What a disgrace my grandma slapped him, since he more likely than not suspected it was I who slapped him. That is really awful, on the grounds that when we get to the following passage, he won't kiss me again.*

"The grandma thinks, That new youngster kissed my granddaughter. *In any case, luckily I brought her up to be a woman, so she slapped him genuine great. I'm happy in light of the fact that presently he'll avoid her when we get to the following tunnel.*

"The overall ponders internally, *I can't completely accept that what simply occurred. I for one handpicked him to be my helper, and I thought he was a genuine courteous fellow. But in the dark, he took advantage of that young girl and kissed her. But she must have thought it was I who kissed her, since I was the one she slapped.*

"In the mean time, I youthful lieutenant is thinking, Boy, that was magnificent. *How frequently do you get to kiss a lovely young lady and slug your supervisor at the equivalent time?*

"The story shows that while four individuals can have similar arrangement of realities, they can come to four distinctive end results. My point is, there is plausible we would all be able to differ on what occurred after we have all of the facts."

"Great relationship," Johnny said, "and sure, it is a clear chance that we may never arrive at a resolution that we can settle on. It would make perfect sense if that is what happens."

"You folks are big cheese leaders," Josh said. "Assuming this were a business circumstance, how might you move toward it? Furthermore please, no committees."

"The main thing we'd do at the bank," said Mark, "would include leading an intensive examination on Mr. Christopher. We'd need to discover all that we could on him. What's more trust me, before the day's over, we'd thoroughly understand him, including what he had for breakfast and his favored image of toothpaste."

"Clearly you're looking at something more broad than running a credit report," Josh joked.

"Precisely. What I have as a main priority will be more on the request for what we'd do assuming we were employing a key leader," Mark answered. "The bank has some great inward individuals, in addition to we contract outside sources that are experts at something like this. In case there is a Mr. Christopher or there has at any point been a Mr. Christopher, when they're through, we'll thoroughly understand him. Trust me
— everything."

"In any event, returning to the 1970s, and with the little data Coach told us?" Josh questioned.

"I've seen examinations return much farther than 28 years," Mark focused with conviction. "In addition, we have a lot of data to direct a careful pursuit. We know the man's last name and that he lived in Bethlehem, and later in Philadelphia."

"His work additionally expected him to come to Ohio," Johnny added.

"Indeed, and I recollect when he was being acquainted with us at The Pep Talk," Josh reviewed. "Didn't Coach say that Mr. Christopher addressed other football crews, including the Cleveland Browns and Philadelphia Eagles?"

"Right, he said that," Mark said in shock. "It seems like we got an adequate number of prompts track down Mr. Christopher."

"How on earth could you be 100% certain?" Josh tested Mark. "We're discussing in excess of a fourth of a century ago."

"I don't have a clue how these folks do it, however our kin are experts at this," Mark said. "Josh, you're the student of history. Look how they research occasions that happened returning centuries."

"Alright, we do a quest for Mr. Christopher," Johnny said. "Furthermore with the utilization of the Internet, I concur, it is possible. Some other ideas?"

"We have some extremely shrewd numbers individuals at the bank," Mark said. "A portion of our folks are splendid mathematicians. I feel sure that when we give them those numbers with our names, they'll make them interest understandings. For example, what are the chances of Mr. Christopher citing Mark 11:24 in a motivational speech before the game, and a player named Mark obstructing eleven passes and making 24 handles? Presently, those chances should be cosmically high. And afterward when it happens two additional occasions with John 20:29 and Joshua 1:9. I'm telling you, the chances should be off the charts."

"While your folks at the bank are doing that," Johnny embedded, "I'll have a portion of our innovation specialists scan the Internet for articles on other sports

occasions that match sacred writing. Absolutely, there will be some match-ups, and provided that this is true, they'll follow up to check whether any are relevant."

"Have them make requests on whether Mr. Christopher or some other person shows up out of the woodwork who conveyed a motivational speech," Mark proposed. "I suggest that they run an inquiry returning to the last part of the 1960s through the present. As outlandish as it sounds, that might be the means by which we track our Mr. Christopher down. We ought not expect that we were the main group that he at any point gave a motivational speech to that had these results."

"Magnificent point," Johnny said. "I believe we're in good shape. What else can we do?"

"I have one," Josh replied. "I suggest that we each record all that we recollect about Mr. Christopher's motivational speech. We'll do it freely, and thereafter, how about we perceive how much our memories match."

"Good thought," Johnny said. "How about we do it over the course of the end of the week so we don't lose any energy. I have a recording device on the plane. I'll begin my recording during my trip to Cape Cod. My secretary will decipher it on Monday."

"You and Mitch can email your memories to me. I'll survey them after the entirety of my considerations are down on paper. Then I'll compare them, and afterward I'll make an attempt to reconstruct The Pep Talk. Wouldn't it be something worth talking about if among us, we can repeat its majority? Wouldn't you like to hear it again?"

"This resembles how the police have a craftsman draw a composite of an individual seen at a crime location by a few observers," added Johnny, his face lighting up.

"I recognized a Radio Shack on Main Street," Mark said. "I'll get a recording device before I hit the road, and I'll record my contemplations on my drive to Columbus."

"Another thing I might want to run by you all," Josh added. "With two children and living on an instructor's compensation and a medical caretaker's pay,my spouse and I battle to earn a living wage. I've been searching for ways of bringing in some additional cash and have even played with composing a book. But so far, I haven't come up with a topic. Presently it resembles a light went off, and I'm feeling that there's some extraordinary material here for my book. In the event that both of you have no protests, I might want to have a go at it. My functioning title will be The Pep Talk."

"Article?" Johnny yelled. "That is a great idea."

"I'm supportive of it as well, Josh," Mark said. "At the point when you review The Pep Talk with our joined information, I am sure you'll have an explosive message. In actuality, I might want to impart it to the bank's supervisory group. You're an understandable man, so I'll stop for a minute, Josh. You review it, and I'll have you be the bank's visitor speaker at a two-day retreat we're having for our top chiefs not long before New Year's in Palm Beach. Do you figure you could be prepared by then?"

"Right? Of course I will. Put me down as your speaker."

"Not really quick, Josh," Johnny interfered. "You really want a specialist. How much will the bank pay Josh, Mitch?"

"I realize we paid last year's speaker 8,000 dollars. That sound OK with you, Josh?"

Josh immediately broadened his right hand. "Shake on that. It's a done deal."

"I wish you wouldn't have acted so quickly, Josh," Johnny said happily. "Assuming you would have allowed me to haggle for you, I might have gotten you 10,000 dollars."

"You do a good job at the retreat," Mark said, "and we'll book you at four more of our division retreats next year, at eight thousand dollars a pop. We're continually searching for inspirational orator, and with this material you'll be a superstar."

"I like your demonstration of approval in me, Mitch, and I could let you down."

"Hello, shouldn't something be said about Alpha Technology? I need you in Orlando toward the beginning of January to talk at our yearly deals meeting," Johnny said."We've as of now reserved a speaker, yet I can add you to the plan. Giving The Pep Talk will start off our new year."

"My chance to be Josh's representative," Mark said. "Josh's talking administrations will cost you 9,000 dollars, Johnny."

"That OK with you, Josh?" Johnny

inquired. "We should shake on it."

"OK, it's an arrangement," Johnny said. "Nine Gs it is. Really awful Mitch didn't allow me to wrap up. I planned to pay you twelve thousand dollars."

The three men giggled and when the check came, Josh said, "Please, the espresso's on me." He smiled and added, "All things considered, I'm fixing to come into some money.

"Yet stand by, another thing. At the point when you send me your memories of The Pep Talk, I'd like you to incorporate how you applied its illustrations all through your professions. For example, Mr. Christopher gabbed about cooperation. Do you recollect how he discussed confiding in everybody to do his assignment?"

"Fantastic thought," Johnny gestured. "I additionally review that Mr. Christopher discussed love. Presently you don't hear that word referenced at the business classes or at the business colleges. I've gone to the board courses at the Harvard Business School, for example, and no one there is conversing with anybody concerning how you should cherish your workers. Having said that, I practice it consistently in my work. I don't walk the floor giving love squeezes to my laborers and letting them know the amount I love them, obviously. In case I did, they'd think I was nuts. But love can be expressed in other ways. I do it by paying them great compensations, giving them incredible incidental advantages and a decent workplace, and by offering them awesome chances for advancement."

"Amen,"Mark said."Love is likewise communicated in the manner in which an administrator recognizes his kin. For instance, I pay attention to individuals. I realize this might seem like something straightforward, however most administrators don't set aside the effort to hear what their kin need to say. Really frequently leaders think they know every one of the appropriate responses and that individuals underneath them aren't savvy enough to let them know anything they don't as of now have a clue. But the truth is, nobody knows their jobs better than the people on the floor who do it eight hours a day, every workday of the year. So in case a chief needs replies, there's the place where he ought to go. His own kin have the appropriate responses. There's no compelling reason to get outside experts; simply pay attention to your own kin. Presently as I would like to think," Mark kept, "listening is a type of showing individuals regard. They feel you regard them since you set aside the effort to hear what they need to say. This isn't excessively complicated. It's great management.

LISTENING IS A FORM
OF SHOWING PEOPLE RESPECT

"A director needs to think often about his kin, and when he does, they react via minding back. Also they take care of their best responsibilities since they would rather not let him down. Like Jesus told us in Mark 10:45, 'The Son of Man came not to be served yet to serve.' I view this section extremely in a serious way since I feel my greatest occupation as CEO is to serve others. Certainly, I realize most managers feel that since they're the boss, they are qualified for be served by their

subordinates. In my mind, they have things confounded. It's the opposite way around. I accept my main need is to serve the workers in my organization. Presently when I serve our directors and they thusly serve others inside the organization, this mentality saturates our association and reaches out past our structure to our clients and providers. The outcome is high representative faithfulness and a lower turnover of individuals, in addition to higher client unwaveringness that thusly creates rehash orders."

Josh began commending. "Right on, right on."

"All things considered, so much for my illustration in Management 101," Mark blushed.

"I concur with all that you say, Mitch," Johnny said. "Jesus committed His life to serving others. This was typified at the Last Supper when He bowed to wash the feet of His supporters. I haven't washed anybody's feet recently, however like you, Mitch, I, as well, accept my occupation as CEO is to serve my people."

"I can see the reason why both of you have been so fruitful," Josh said. "Kindly make certain to incorporate how you apply the examples from The Pep Talk in your business vocations when you send your memories to me. I trust that the message from Mr. Christopher's motivational speech was expected to remain with us long after we quit playing football. Presently we are liable for giving it to others."

"Say, Josh, while no doubt about it," Mark said, "when you review The Pep Talk for your talk, I'd like it in case you could make a rundown that sums up its significant illustrations. I'll utilize the rundown as a secret when I converse with my promoting individuals about your presentation."

"Consider it done," Josh said. "I'll send a duplicate to you as well, Johnny." "Amazing. Presently if it's all the same to you, fellas, we should wrap this up," Johnny said.

"Mitch will have an expert examination led on Mr.   Christopher to see what we can uncover on him. Also assuming he's as yet fit as a fiddle, we'll check whether we can converse with him. Concurred? Great. Second, Mitch has his mathematical folks run the numbers so we know the probabilities of something like this occurrence. Third, my innovation folks at Alpha will do a broad pursuit, both on some other extraordinary motivational speeches previously, and for different games articles that may make references identifying with Scripture. Maybe if we do enough digging, we'll discover that this isn't as uncommon as it appears to be. At long last, Josh will recreate The Pep Talk dependent on each of our memories of it."

"We should not let an excess of grass develop under our feet before we meet once more," Mark said. "Really take a look at your schedules the primary thing on Monday morning, and if

you both can work it in, how about we go for the end of the prior week Thanksgiving when we get together. I recommend that we meet in Columbus, which obviously is advantageous for Josh and me. Accomplishes that work for you, Johnny?"

"I'll make it work," Johnny answered.

On the manner in which home from their gathering, Josh's drive appeared to be extensively more limited. It was a similar distance, yet this time the secondary school history instructor was riding on a clear high. Indeed, assuming he could tackle the adrenalin shooting through his veins at the present time, Josh realized he would have sufficient energy to fuel a 747. He could scarcely hold back his fervor. He was thrilled with the gathering with his lifelong companions, and enchanted with the secret of Mr. Christopher.

What daily. Under six hours prior his greatest concern was paying for his girl's orthodontia. Presently, Josh's cash issues would before long be behind him. It was a magnificent, unimaginable help. He could scarcely hold back to break the news to Sarah, however there was a lot of rustic Ohio around him for his phone to get gathering. Josh would essentially need to delay until he was in range. At last, nearby Columbus, Josh speed-dialed her so he could transfer what all had happened on this most noteworthy day.

"Howdy, honey," Sarah said. "You should be depleted. I need to hear about your day, yet before you enlighten me regarding it, I make them energize news that I'm kicking the bucket to tell you. First of all, I have some work working nights at The Limited among Thanksgiving and Christmas. Second, I conversed with Dr. Sharp and I inquired as to whether we could pay for Maggie's supports in portions. We talked for some time, and he concurred we could pay $222.22 every month for the following three years, and with no interest. I can barely handle it. Is it safe to say that he is the most delightful man? Presently can your uplifting news top that?"

"Indeed, first off," Josh replied, "you can tell Dr. Sharp that we profoundly like his liberality. Yet, in case he'll be adequately thoughtful to delay until mid-January,we'll simply take care of him in full."

"I'm not after you, Josh," she answered. "Except if you won the lottery today, precisely how would you propose we concoct 8,000 dollars by mid-January?"

"In light of the fact that by then, at that point, my caring spouse, our cash issues will be behind us."

"It sounds awesome, sweetheart," Sarah answered, "and as you can envision, I am very keen on realizing what has ended up making that conceivable. Did you run over a since a long time ago, lost relative in Lincoln who is exceptionally rich and of whom I have no knowledge?"

"It's a boring tale, Sarah, yet here goes . . ." Josh began.

PIECING TOGETHER
THE PUZZLE

Josh Goldman spent most of the day on Saturday putting together what he remembered about The Pep Talk. He was surprised at how much he retained over the past three decades. All together he had twelve pages of single-spaced notes, which included two pages about how he applied lessons from The Pep Talk to his teaching position. He wondered if Johnny and Mitch could have possibly matched what he was able to summon up. Sarah read his notes and was astonished that he could recall so much detail. She was similarly dazzled with the content.

"This is magnificent material," she remarked. "It has a directive for everybody. Honestly, I was expecting a type of run of the mill motivational speech that I envisioned mentors provided for their players before a game. This is nothing similar to I anticipated. The medical clinic directors could unquestionably apply this message. Also the specialists I work with, kid do they need it."

"Would you be able to perceive how any of Mr. Christopher's motivational speech has come off on me?" he asked sheepishly.

"I absolutely can," she said, adding, "Mr. Ohio Teacher of the Year."

"Seriously, honey. Tell me something concrete."

"All things considered, first of all, you live by Mr. Christopher's words when he told the group to 'hold onto the day.' Indeed you live by the way of thinking that directs: 'This is my day, and I will make the most out of it.'"

"Do you truly feel that is My specialty?" Josh asked timidly. "Totally,"

Sarah proceeded. "This way of thinking is profoundly engrained in

your cerebrum. You even stroll around singing the verses to Tim McGraw's song,

'Live Like You Were Dying'— the one with regards to the man in his mid forties who just got X-beams from the specialist and has been told he's dying.

"Definitely, I love that he never surrendered!" said Josh, with recharged fervor. "Truth be told, he ascended mountains, leaped out of planes, and went fishing when

he might have straightforwardly surrendered. But instead, he decided to enjoy all the things he had taken for granted, like his family and his friends, and to live each day as it came—never knowing if it might be his last."

"And how often have I heard you remark on the articulation 'Today is the main day of the remainder of your life,' saying that you'd favor individuals to pose the inquiry, 'Imagine a scenario where today was the last day of your life?'"

"Better believe it, I do say that a lot. What else?"

"I've heard you recount to that tale about the heavenly man and the scorpion somewhere multiple times," she said, "and how often do you utilize the articulation a while later, 'This is the thing that I do'?"

"I guess I have said that now and again, and indeed, I guess I got it The Pep Talk. Anything else?"

"I really accept that you're a particularly brilliant instructor since you expect such a large amount your understudies," she replied. "You set an exclusive expectation for them, and thusly, they will quite often overachieve so they will not baffle you."

Sarah stopped and embraced her better half. "Guarantee me that you'll never quit any pretense of educating, on the grounds that it genuinely is your calling."

"I guarantee you, honey. I'll generally be an instructor," Josh guaranteed her. "Since—to cite myself—'this is the thing that I do.'"

When Josh checked his email on Monday evening, his messages from Johnny and Mark were holding back to be opened. The two men appended since

quite a while ago, point by point records. His two companions had progressed nicely; Johnny sent thirteen single-divided composed pages; Mitch had a fifteen-page report, likewise perfectly introduced. According to their expert looking arrangements he received
— mistake free—Josh inferred that his two companions had clearly assigned the composing to a right hand. Obviously, he had composed and composed his report himself. Subsequent to printing the archives, Josh laid them alongside his and started collaborating. He was bewildered to see how comparable the archives were. Despite the fact that he had no chance of knowing it, their consolidated endeavors had covered all that Mr. Christopher had said to the team.

Studying the three archives, he was excited to find that The Pep Talk had significantly more meat to it than he had expected. Josh accepted its

message was not planned to be given uniquely to secondary school football players—it contained significant examples to have the option to prevail in any undertaking. He was likewise persuaded that its message could be conveyed to a full grown crowd. Josh would reproduce it from their notes in general, and when it was finished, he would be ready to fill in as its courier to the world. Josh unexpectedly felt as though he had a mission throughout everyday life, similar as he did when he accepted his first educating task. He could feel the passion. It was wonderful.

SURROUND YOURSELF WITH ENTHUSIASTIC PEOPLE.

Regarding the matter of passion, Johnny dedicated almost a full page to how The Pep Talk had terminated him up and, subsequently, how it had propelled him to play at a max execution all through the whole game. He stressed how he and his partners had played the round of their lives. "At the point when I talk with likely possibility for key administrative positions," his notes uncovered, "I search for people who have this quality. I accept it is so fundamental in the working environment that I've been known to enlist an applicant with passion however with a less noteworthy list of references rather than a more qualified individual who does not have this quality. In all honesty, I have an antipathy for tepid individuals. I like to be encircled with individuals who are excited and have passion."

When Josh read Johnny's remark about passion, he recollected how the players clasped turns in the clusters. He reviewed how Johnny continued to move everybody to be completely centered around his task. "Be so engaged you can peruse the letters ready as it twistings into your hands," he told his beneficiaries. "Ace your container," he energized every hostile lineman.

"Everybody take care of your task," he rehashed all through the game.

Reading Johnny's notes, Josh reviewed John 20:29: "Favored are the individuals who have not seen but then have come to accept." Remembering Mr. Christopher rehashing this sacred text to the group, Josh understood that Johnny's authority during the game embodied the significance of this stanza. As the group's quarterback, Johnny roused the hostile unit to work collectively, confiding in every player to execute his task, and together they beat a generally predominant adversary. Johnny's faith in his linemen—confiding in them to shield him against the greater, more grounded Jacktown players—roused them to accept they could beat their rival. He accepted they could do what they had never had the option to do. His confidence gave them confidence in

themselves. They would have rather not frustrate him since he trusted in them.

Similarly, in the business field, this equivalent brand of initiative enabled Johnny to establish and assemble Alpha Technology, an organization that at last

developed into a significant innovative organization. Here as well, Johnny put stock in the inconspicuous. Josh pondered how Johnny had fabricated Alpha without any preparation, and he imagined how his companion confronted and conquered apparently unconquerable snags en route. How troublesome it probably been in the early phases to persuade fit individuals to surrender safer positions where they were utilized to join his little new business. Considering the number of new businesses fail from the start, he thought of it as amazing that they would do as such without any affirmations that Alpha would some time or another make due, not to mention thrive.

Equally troublesome was the assignment of fund-raising from financial backers, convincing them to put resources into an organization without a history. Clearly to prevail upon representatives and financial backers, they needed to have confidence in Alpha's future—and in particular in Johnny Corleone. They needed to put stock in the image of things to come that Johnny painted. *This is the thing that solid initiative is*, Josh gathered. Three cheers for his companion Johnny Corleone, originator and CEO of Alpha Technology!

Mark composed a solitary divided page exposition on responsibility In business, a significant example that he took from The Pep Talk and applied all through his whole profession. "Like a football crew," he stated, "in each association every part adds to the entire, and each fruitful result should be ascribed to the individuals in general." He went on to explain how every department has its own area of responsibility, and the success of the entire organization depends on the combined performances of all departments.

Assuming one part isn't finishing their task, it influences the whole office. "In the event that, for example, the salespeople are delivering enormous orders, what benefit is it assuming the plant falls behind on creation and can't satisfy orders? The equivalent is valid in the event that the bookkeeping office neglects to send solicitations or gather installments due the organization. Each person and each division should be considered responsible. In business, everybody should arrange; an all out collaboration is required."

Josh seen how each of them three expounded on the significance of having faith in a positive result. "Never view your opposition as a monster, and in examination, consider yourself to be a grasshopper," Johnny composed. Mark cited Joshua 1:9: "Be solid and gallant; don't be terrified or

overwhelmed; for the LORD your God is with you any place you go." Here, Mark underlined how he accepted that with God on his side, he will undoubtedly prevail in all undertakings. *What a superb disposition*, Josh thought. "No big surprise Mitch does as such well," he recounted to Sarah.

Mark reviewed the tale about the undergrad who had the option to tackle the two issues his teacher composed on the class board that even puzzled Albert Einstein. Mark pushed, "The fact of the matter is, you can accomplish anything you accept you can accomplish. At the point when I began at the bank, I accepted I could achieve each advancement that I in the end got. Presently, when I began at a low section level, I wasn't figuring how I would sometime be the bank's CEO. Rather I put my focus on turning into an associate branch administrator, and when I got that advancement, I centered doing what was important to turn into the branch chief. I did this all through my profession when I turned into an area administrator, a provincial supervisor, right hand VP, VP, etc as I moved gradually up the company pecking order. While it's something positive to prepare to stun the world, I zeroed in on with extra special care. That is what Mr. Christopher taught us to do—center around each play, each in turn. Had we just been centered around the scoreboard, we wouldn't have practiced our given tasks on every individual play. The equivalent is pertinent in business."

Mark expounded that under his direction State National had a ground breaking strategy to extend by obtaining banks in unassuming communities all through Ohio. Also, it intended to gain little and medium-sized local banks. "Here, as well, it was each obtaining in turn. Or then again as Mr. Christopher said, 'Each play in turn, and the scoreboard will deal with itself.' I generally thought past the present into the future, and I was never engrossed with transient benefits. In business, there are times when it is important to bring about transient misfortunes so that drawn out gains can be realized."

RUN ONE PLAY AT A TIME, AND THE FINAL SCORE
WILL TAKE CARE OF ITSELF.

Josh accurately surveyed Mr. Christopher's motivational speech as an example on confronting affliction. It had a more profound significance than setting up a football crew to confront a great adversary any semblance of the Jacktown Giants. He had advised the players to expect misfortune in the game, that they would confront it together, and above all, they would be there for one another. He focused on that realizing they were in good company and could trust each other would fill in as a source of

strength; together they could defeat their adversary.

SUCCESS IS GOING FROM FAILURE
TO FAILURE WITHOUT FAILING.

The group's definitive success over Jacktown would remain with them for a lifetime. It was unmistakable evidence that it is feasible to defy outlandish chances and be successful. Having encountered an accomplishment of this size at an early age was for sure a gift. *There is nothing similar to learning a significant example by really doing it,* Josh thought to himself.

The 24 game losing mark that his group experienced before its triumph over Jacktown likewise streaked to him. He wondered about the way that the group could be wrecked—actually no, wrecked, yet squashed—many games and still suit up and face next Friday night's adversary. *That is the thing that makes football such a dynamite sport,* he considered. *Each play brings about little youngsters getting wrecked, and thereafter, they should take themselves off the ground despite the fact that they might be knockeddown once more.* This without anyone else is a great illustration in life since life itself is a progression of many losses. Versatility is a great attribute to gain as a youngster. The mystery of achievement, Josh recorded in his notes, is to have the capacity to suffer a large number of losses without permitting yourself to be crushed. One more method for saying it, he thought, would be: Success is going from one inability to another without failing.

By the center of the week, Josh had recreated the whole motivational speech and sent it to Johnny and Mark. His email additionally incorporated a rundown of twelve significant illustrations contained in The Pep Talk:

1. Don't overcome yourself before you get everything rolling by permitting negative musings about previous occasions trouble you with limits. As Carl Sandburg expressed, "The past is a can of cinders." Rid yourself of self-question. Try not to permit yourself to be crushed by preconceptions.

2. Seize the occasion. In a critical second you can decide to say, "This is my day, and I will capitalize on it."

3. Nobody prevails without the assistance of others. It requires a collaboration. Trust

others to take care of their responsibilities. The joined exertion of everybody executing their work produces prevalent results.

4. Stay centered. Try not to zero in on the scoreboard; the last score will deal with itself. In business, don't be engrossed with how much cash you will make. Focus on your job that needs to be done—the cash will come.

5. Visualize your prosperity. This will give you an objective that you will ultimately attain.

6. Adversity is important forever. Try not to allow difficulties to overcome you. Difficulty makes you stronger.

7. Be diligent. Never, never give in.

8. Expect the opposition to be solid. Try not to underrate an opponent.

9. Believe in others and others will put stock in you.

10. Be a group player.

11. Believe and trust the interaction. Free yourself of self-doubts.

12. Believe you will succeed. Have confidence in your future (the unseen).

On Thursday evening Josh got a call from Johnny Corleone. "Congrats on working really hard," Johnny said to him. "I felt like I was paying attention to Mr. Christopher when I read it. Also your rundown of the twelve significant illustrations was flawless. Incidentally, I had a significant conversation with Stan Howard, our VP of Marketing and told him everything—Mr. Christopher's motivational speech, the game, last week's get-together with Coach Morris in Lincoln, and what the three of us are doing concerning the re-production of The Pep Talk. He's as amped up for all of this as we are. He put you in the program to address our outreach group in Orlando on January 19, Saturday morning at 10:30. He needs you to represent 45 minutes. Accomplishes that work for you?"

"Great," Josh replied.

"Gracious indeed, I ventured to have Katie Wilson,my leader aide, book a reservation for you withdrawing Columbus early Friday evening. I accept you are anticipating bringing Sarah, so Katie booked her as well. You are bringing her, aren't you, Josh?"

"I will, and I realize how excited she'll be," Josh replied.

"Katie held a space for you at Four Seasons. I'm looking forward to meeting Sarah."

"Hello, before you hang up," Josh asked, "what did your math wonders concoct with respect to the probabilities?"

"They're actually chipping away at it," Johnny said, "so we'll need to sit back and watch. They're additionally doing look on the Internet to check whether they can observe articles that have scriptural references. They've gone over a large number of them, so they're looking at them, individually. It will require some investment to check whether any are significant. I'll update you as often as possible. Ciao."

As soon as Josh put down the collector, he raced into the kitchen to tell Sarah, "Johnny Corleone affirmed that I will be talking in Orlando on January 19."

"Thank you, dear God," Sarah said, accepting her better half, her eyes looking skyward.

"The charges from the discourse alone cover Maggie's supports," Josh answered, giving her a major press. "Gracious, another thing. You're going too."

Two hours after the fact Mark called. "I apologize for hitting you up at such an inconvenient time, Josh, yet when Janie perceived how invigorated I was the point at which I returned home this evening, she needed to know why, so I educated her concerning The Pep Talk. Then she insisted that I read it to her after dinner. Janie and I are both overjoyed with regards to how you managed our notes. It's very amazing work. We have something exceptionally unique here, my friend."

"I'm excited you like it so much," Josh said.

"Coincidentally, our kin have begun their examination on Mr. Christopher. No leads starting today, yet recollect, persistence is an ideals. Assuming that he's out there, they'll find him.

"Another thing," Mark added. "Before I left the workplace I conversed with my VP who's accountable for the retreat we're having toward the year's end. I let him know I needed you to address our supervisory crew. Mark December 28 and 29 on your schedule, Josh. That is the Tuesday and Wednesday among Christmas and New Year's. You said you could make it. I'm trusting that works for you."

"Most certainly," Josh said excitedly.

"It's at The Breakers in Palm Beach. Somebody from the bank will call you in a day or so with the details."

"Superb," Josh said.

Everything was starting to become all-good for Josh Goldman. His cash issues would before long be behind him. He was gaining incredible ground with the composition of The Pep Talk. And, perhaps best of all, Josh had a new lease on life because he felt that what he was doing would have a positive influence on the lives of many people. "Life is useful for this Ohio teacher," he told his better half, Sarah.

On Friday evening, November 26, Josh got an email from Johnny Corleone:

Josh,

> Mitch and I shared any useful info on what we looked into Mr. Christopher and his motivational speech. We need to do a telephone gathering with you and Coach Morris on Wednesday evening, December 1. Does 7:30 next Wednesday work for you? Assuming this is the case, I'll set up a phone call. Tell me. Anticipating conversing with you.

Johnny

On December 1, 2003, the video chat started instantly at 7:30 p.m. "Before we get everything rolling," Johnny said, "I trust all of you had a wonderful Thanksgiving. How was yours, Coach?"

"My little girls and their families visited," Morris answered in a slight voice. "We are honored with lovely youngsters and grandchildren."

"I'm here as well," Margaret Morris ringed in. "I trust you young men wouldn't fret. Jack needed me to tune in so in the event that he missed something, I'd recollect it for him."

"SMart thought, Mrs. M, and it's consistently a joy to hear your voice. I'm glad to hear all of you partook in your Thanksgiving," Johnny said energetically. Then, changing hats and sounding very much like a CEO, he explained to Margaret and Jack Morris about how the three of them had stopped at the diner and what they discussed. He likewise brought them state-of-the-art on the

examinations that were being directed by both Alpha and State National. "As may be obvious, we were as charmed with what you told us as you were, Coach, and we needed to check whether there was some consistent clarification to every last bit of it. The motivation behind this telephone call is to refresh you on what we learned."

Johnny halted in his idea and said, "Mitch, I don't intend to rule this discussion. So how about you give your report first, and thereafter I'll circle back to mine."

"I'll be charmed," Mark contributed. "As all of you know, our bank should be familiar with individuals we advance cash to. I alloted Peter Jefferson, perhaps our best individual at State National, to discover all that there was to be aware of Mr. Christopher. I gave Jefferson the data we had some awareness of Mr. Christopher, which in fact was definitely not a ton, however when I initially gave this data to him he said, 'This is all that could possibly be needed, Mark. Simply allow me daily or two, and I'll have a lot to answer to you about the man.'"

"Excuse me, briefly, Mitch," Johnny said, "however didn't Jefferson let you know that these days, making reference to the Internet, that it would be a stroll in the park?"

"In those exact words," Mark concurred. "Now like I said, Peter Jefferson has a reputation for being an outstanding investigator. Five days later Jefferson told me, 'I'm not finding anything on this guy, Mr. Mitchell, but don't you worry, something's got to show up. I have a call into a contact in Philly who promised to get back to me on Monday. If a Mr. Christopher ever existed, we'll soon know all about him.' Well, Jefferson and his associate in Philadelphia didn't come up with jack squat. Finally last week, Jefferson threw in the towel. He told me, 'Mr. Mitchell, it's as if the man never existed. I've never seen anything like it in my entire career, nor for that matter, have any of my colleagues.' So that's my final report. Nada!"

"Much thanks," Morris said, his voice sounding somewhat more grounded. "Like I told you young men, while I'm not a specialist like the bank's man, I ran into exactly the same thing when I attempted to contact Mr. Christopher.

Maybe he never existed.”

“What happened when Jefferson checked with the Philadelphia Eagles and Cleveland Browns?” Josh inquired. “Did anybody remember a Mr. Christopher or a more interesting giving a kick talk?”

“No one recalled anything,” Mark replied. “Yet, faculty in the two groups said there have been many,many visitor speakers throughout the long term, and

with the turnover of players and mentors, no one is around from when Mr. Christopher may have given a motivational speech to one or the other group. Furthermore, neither one of the associations kept any records of visitor speakers from up until this point back.”

“Presently, for my discoveries,” Johnny said. “I do have some substantial outcomes to answer to you. As the three of us concurred at the cafe, I elected to allot a portion of my mathematicians at Alpha to decide the probabilities of a man citing sacred texts before a football match-up was played that were applicable to the names, players’ numbers, and playing insights in the genuine game. I’m alluding to those articles that you showed us, Coach, when you featured Mark 11:24, John 20:29, and Joshua 1:9. Is everybody with me?”

He stopped and sat tight for their consent. “Great. I could give you arrangements of raw numbers, yet to spare the gritty details, the chances were so cosmically high, there were no chances,” Johnny proceeded. “We’re discussing billions to one. I needed to twofold actually take a look at this, so I reached Bill Brown, a companion of mine who’s a prominent statistician at Travelers. Indeed, he also concocted nothing. Believe it or not, zip. Nada. What’s more he offered no clarification. Not taking care of business of confidence, Brown wouldn’t completely accept that what had occurred. He basically reasoned that it was outlandish. To cite him word for word: ‘It isn’t workable for an individual to forecast what you guarantee your Mr. Christopher did.’ He demanded that the scriptural statements couldn’t have been made before the game and said that The Pep Talk needed to have been made a short time later. It simply was preposterous, and what without a doubt happened was that we got the dates wrong.

“‘Something is unmistakably missing that you’re not telling me.’ he kept up with. ‘I’m not recommending that it was deliberate. However, a portion of the realities have been omitted.’

“Oh yes, he then went on to say something we had wondered about earlier: ‘The Pep Talk quoted John 15:12, but there was no reference to it in any of the newspaper articles. Absolutely, this should excite your doubts? Assuming this was, as you propose, God-propelled, for what reason wasn't there a player named John with relating numbers 15 and 12 that were additionally relevant? Got you there, don't I?' he said."

"I've been contemplating that myself," Josh said.

"What's more what did you close?" Johnny

asked.

"My interpretation of it is," Josh replied, "that assuming we trust in God, we shouldn't anticipate that He should need to substantiate Himself. So what occurred here is that a piece of the riddle is deliberately absent. Assuming God needed us to have absolute,

evident verification of His reality, we would have had it millennia ago."

"So be it," Morris said.

"I might want to proceed with my report," Johnny said. "Being that Alpha is in the innovative business and we approach the top Internet organizations, I had a portion of my kin check with our sources to see what may show up in regards to another football match-up or another game that may take after our experience. Indeed, they concocted scriptural names like John, Peter, Samuel, Jeremiah, Daniel, etc. They looked at them all. They even observed a few parts and stanzas that matched numbers relating to game measurements. Considering the huge quantities of games played throughout the long term, going in we figured that will undoubtedly occur. Furthermore on certain events there were games with sacred writings coordinating players' names with their shirt number just as their game measurements. Those leads were likewise followed up however created no unmistakable outcomes. There was never more than one in a solitary game. So they credited that to the law of probabilities—never with a Mr. Christopher.

"Now you have to remember, their search only went from the present back to the mid-1950s, a relatively short period of time," Johnny continued. "It would be presumptuous to assume that a similar incident or incidents could not have occurred centuries ago and certainly at a different venue. Instead of on a football field, it could have been on a battlefield, in a debate at the League of Nations, or even on the Roman Senate floor. Perhaps there have been many 'Mr. Christophers,' who came in different attire. Rather than wearing a business suit and a fedora, they wore cloaks, or for that matter, dresses or gowns. Perhaps it was a 'Ms. Christopher' who delivered the message."

"I concur," Josh interposed. "It would be pompous for us to feel that what occurred at The Pep Talk would be the main arrangement where a peculiarity of this nature could happen. Absolutely, we need to give credit to the Good

Lord for being creative."

Josh snickered at what he recently said. "That is interesting. All things considered, God is our Supreme Creator. Is there any good reason why He wouldn't be innovative?"

"All things considered, folks, to this end it took such a long time, on the grounds that at first they restricted their hunt to football match-ups," Johnny added, "and nothing came up that had to do with a motivational speech or whatever else that might actually prediction such exact

measurements before a game. Nor did anything appear that had a say in Mr. Christopher. Then they started to explore other avenues and again, they drew a blank. Taking everything into account, they inferred that this was a unique event—that is, with respect to a motivational speech and a football match-up or a game. But when you look at the big picture— over the centuries, there is no way of investigating events that were never recorded."

"Thank you kindly," Morris said. "This implies such a great amount

to me." "We love you, Coach, yet we did it for us as well," Mitch

said.

"We additionally have an unexpected treat for you, Coach," Johnny said. "The three of us autonomously recorded all that we recall about Mr. Christopher's Pep Talk, and Josh, being the history specialist in our group, re-made it from all of our recollections."

"You did?" Morris said. "Would i be able to have a copy?"

"When I've finished it, Coach," Josh replied. "I believe it's essentially similar to what Mr. Christopher said. This moment, it's a work in progress and in its subsequent draft. I'll complete my third and last draft by Friday."

"In two days? That is magnificent," Morris said.

"I'll for the time being it to you for a Saturday conveyance," Josh replied.

"All things considered, what would be the best next step; what does this all mean?" Margaret Morris inquired. "What's more what might be said about Mr. Christopher? We don't know anything about him. Also what might be said about those billions-to-one odds?"

"I decide to accept it was God-motivated," Mark said.

"Mitch is correct," Jack Morris said. "I'm not sure how this all occurred, yet I have confidence that there is a justification for why it occurred. Furthermore that is adequate for me. For a man in my condition, I can't see you how soothing that is. All of this reconfirms my conviction that I have something magnificent to anticipate when I am presently not of this earth."

"God favor you young men," Margaret Morris said.

On Saturday morning, December 4, 2003, Jack Morris got the primary duplicate of The Pep Talk. In spite of the fact that no one could at any point know, it was indistinguishable, in exactly the same words, to what Mr. Christopher had said.

Jack Morris was sitting in his cowhide seat behind his work area in his library. He had nodded off with his right hand gripping the last page from The Pep Talk. Margaret looked in the room and was glad to see the substance articulation on his face.

THE PEP TALK REVISITED

On December 28, 2003, Mark Mitchell, CEO of State National Bank, stood at the podium in a conference room at The Breakers Hotel in Palm Beach, Florida. He was addressing thirty-six senior managers at a early daytime meeting. It was an energetic gathering, and Mark was great at terminating them up.

"Good day," he welcomed them. "I'm enchanted to be with you today in radiant Florida." Mark talked for a couple of moments about bank business. He then announced, "I am privileged to have the honor of introducing our guest speaker, Josh Goldman, who I promise will tell you something that will be nothing like anything you've ever heard before. My companion Josh and I go way back. We experienced childhood in Lincoln, Ohio, a little previous steel plant town close to the Pennsylvania and West Virginia borders. Lincoln High was once likewise known for its stalwart football crews. But that was way back in the '50s when most of us in this room were not even born.

"During the '70s when Josh and I were Lincoln Lions partners," Mark proceeded, "our group was no force to be reckoned with. At one time, we were riding a 24 game losing streak and were confronting the Jacktown Giants—and to us they truly were monsters. They had a 42 game series of wins and were the state champions for three successive years. But something unusual happened the night before, and we did win that game in undoubtedly the biggest upset in Ohio high school football history."

Mark proceeded to educate his crowd concerning the more peculiar who had conversed with the group the night prior to the game. He gave a summary of the actual game. He was not modest with regards to informing them concerning his eleven broken passes and 24 handles. He additionally discussed Johnny finishing twenty out of 29 passes, and pointing a finger at the visitor speaker, he depicted how Josh kicked three field objectives, incorporating the triumphant one with three seconds staying on the clock. Mark likewise had the news cut-outs of the game projected on a screen. Then he showed them copies that had been

featured and clarified how these numbers compared with the sacred writing cited in The Pep Talk. Next he clarified how specialists determined the probabilities in the billions and how they couldn't track down the outsider despite having what ought to have been abundant data to find him. At last, he portrayed the effect that The Pep Talk had on his life just as on Johnny's and Josh's.

"I'll simply say another thing before our visitor speaker addresses everyone," Mark said. "Assuming it were not really for Mr. Christopher's motivational speech, I am sure that my life would have been very different." He stopped momentarily and added, "I genuinely accept that I wouldn't be remaining here today as the CEO of this organization notwithstanding The Pep Talk."

By the time Mark had gotten done, his crowd was as eager and anxious as ever. "Lovely people, I present to you my old buddy Josh Goldman who will convey The Pep Talk as it has been re-made by Josh, Johnny, and yours genuinely. And keeping in mind that we at State National may not be a football crew, I guarantee you that its message will be as motivating and significant to you as it has been to us."

Josh strolled to the platform and stood confronting the crowd, trusting that the commendation will fade away. At the point when the room was quiet, he said: "There were two bison remaining in the open reach in Wyoming . . ."

12 BUSINESS LESSONS
FROM THE PEP TALK

1. Don't overcome yourself before you get everything rolling by permitting negative contemplations about previous occasions trouble you with impediments. As Carl Sandburg expressed, "The past is a container of remains." Rid yourself of self-question. Try not to permit yourself to be crushed by preconceptions.

2. Seize the occasion. In a vital second you can decide to say, "This is my day, and I will take advantage of it."

3. Nobody prevails without the assistance of others. It requires a collaboration. Trust others to go about their responsibilities. The joined exertion of everybody executing their work produces predominant results.

4. Stay centered. Try not to zero in on the scoreboard; the last score will deal with itself. In business, don't be distracted with how much cash you will make. Focus on your main job—the cash will come.

5. Visualize your prosperity. This will give you an objective that you will ultimately attain.

6. Adversity is essential forever. Try not to allow mishaps to overcome you. Affliction makes you stronger.

7. Be persevering. Never, never give in.

8. Expect the opposition to be solid. Try not to misjudge an opponent.

9. Believe in others and others will have faith in you.

10. Be a group player.

11. Believe and trust the interaction. Free yourself of self-doubts.

12. Believe you will succeed. Have confidence in your future (the concealed).